Fragments from a Land of Freedom

Fragments from a Land of Freedom

Essays on American Culture
around the Year 2000

Paolo L. Bernardini

Washington, DC

Copyright © 2010 by Paolo L. Bernardini

New Academia Publishing, 2010

All rights reserved. No part of this book may be reproduced or transmitted in any form or by any means, electronic or mechanical, including photocopying, recording, or by any information storage and retrieval system.

Printed in the United States of America

Library of Congress Control Number: 2010934190
ISBN 978-0-9794488-9-8 paperback (alk. paper)

 An imprint of new Academia Publishing
P.O. Box 27420 - Washington, DC 20008

 info@newacademia.com - www.newacademia.com

To Norman Fiering
Director of the John Carter Brown Library
at Brown University
from 1983 to 2004
in friendship

America makes prodigious mistakes, America has colossal faults, but one thing cannot be denied: America is always on the move. She may be going to Hell, of course, but at least she isn't standing still.

E.E. Cummings

America's greatest strength, and its greatest weakness, is our belief in second chances, our belief that we can always start over, that things can be made better.

Anthony Walton

Contents

Foreword to the English Edition   xi
Aknowledgments   xiv
Introduction   xv

I. On African-Americans, Native Americans, and Jews (and more)   1
    African-American Destinies   3
    The Lost Footprints of Sand Creek   7
    Bad Blue Blood: New York Jewish Aristocracy   11
    The Road to Refuge   15
    The Holocaust at Battery Park   21
    Following the Hutterites   29

II. On Men, Poets, and Presidents (and not only)   35
    Parallel Deaths   37
    The "Great Experiment" Called the U.S.A.   41
    The True Story of Uncle Sam   45
    Disability and Poetry: A Homage to Vassar Miller   49
    An American Sphinx   55

III. On Knowledge, Learning and Understanding (men and places)   67
    In the Enchanted Forest of Knowledge   69
    A Look Towards Europe   73
    To School, for What?   77

The Infinite Gardens of Mr. and Mrs. Huntington	83
Anthropology of Power: The Death of Eric R. Wolf	89
A Chair Named After Albert O. Hirschman	95
Brandeis at Fifty	103
The Rich, the Poor, and David S. Landes	109
IV. On Wars and Other Places (in peace)	**123**
Once Upon a Time There was Vietnam	125
Caravaggio in the Balkans	129
In Hiroshima's Shadow	133
The Beautiful Summer of Son of Sam	137
Atlantic City: Gambling at a Fever Pitch	141
A Day in the Life of Philadelphia	145
Vienna in New York	151
Index of Names	159

Foreword to the English Edition

This book was conceived and written during the 1998-1999 academic year, and was published in Italian in 2001. After the completion of its English translation (which included the re-writing of several chapters and the re-thinking of the entire work), in 2009-10, I felt the need to add this short preface to the original introduction.

We live in an age in which nine years can be regarded as a very long lapse of time. I wrote this book during the last period of President Bill Clinton's second term. The USA was extremely cautious in its foreign policy and 9/11 could not have been fathomed in America's future.

It was also a time of prosperity, although the major crisis which affected the stock market and thus the whole American and international economy was lurking, and there were signs of its coming.

The U.S., in books, exhibits, cultural events, and other manifestations of its identity and civilization (as they are described and commented in this book) was calmly reconsidering its past and its place in the world, especially after the collapse of Soviet Communism.

9/11 and the events that followed, including the invasion of Afghanistan and Iraq, the ongoing war on terrorism, and the shift from a Democratic to a Republican administration, offered Americans a renewed desire to reshape their sense of identity, as well as a more immediate urge to act as a primary agent in global policies.

The value of this book consists in depicting a world on the verge of a profound change.

On a personal note, many things changed in my life after I spent that wonderful year at the Institute for Advanced Study in Princeton, where I wrote these twenty-six cultural essays.

After moving around the world to study and teach for a few years, I finally settled down as director of the Center for Italian and European Studies of Boston University in Padova, Italy. Eventually, I left that position for a chair in European History at the University of Insubria in Como, Italy, a newly created state college, with a great potential for growth, being as it is placed in one of the richest and most beautiful parts of Northern Italy.

While directing the Boston University Center in Padova, I taught American students and I witnessed their astonishment when I informed them of the terrorist attacks on the Twin Towers. This forced me to reconsider my "classical liberal" views of politics and society, and to endorse the "minimal state" concept, embracing the libertarian ideas of thinkers such as Mises and Rothbard. In March 2005, a couple of months before I wrote this preface, I had the honor of visiting the Ludwig von Mises Institute in Auburn, Alabama. I was admitted as a member of the adjunct faculty, for which I deeply thank Lew Rockwell Jr, its president.

My political ideas substantially changed, since I published the Italian edition of this book. I did not change, however, the contents of the book for this American edition, almost a decade later.

While re-reading and revising these essays for publication in English, I realized, *ex post*, how they convey a pleasant, tranquil, rather unproblematic image of the USA. It seems to be a country – in reading these essays – that came to terms with its troubled past, and was able to confront the most problematic, unhappy pages of its history. Nothing around the year 2000 warned us of the economic catastrophes that occurred after 2001, and the political upheaval caused by 9/11—two wars of invasion were certainly not looming on the horizon when I wrote these essays. Thus, I tend to see this work as a picture of peace through a wide angle lens: America's, and mankind's, last happy days before a major, epoch-making crisis.

These essays show, first and foremost, the destiny of peoples and individuals as they evolved on the major background of a mighty nation and a stormy history. If America is the place where great individuals might emerge and fulfill the "American dream", or rather, the "American prophecy" (be yourself, be honest, and prosper), that case is definitely made in this book. The opposite case, however, is made as well: the case of the dialectics between individual(s) and society, a struggle which often ends up with the latter's victory. While writing these essays, I also realized that a book meant for the Italian public could also be of interest to the English-speaking public, including the American reader, who would see familiar history from the perspective of a foreign observer.

The title of the book, in its original Italian edition, is *A Sphinx without a Secret"**, adapted from a well-known short story by Oscar Wilde. The story describes a beautiful lady who apparently hides some secrets. But, actually, those secrets do not exist. The United States can be seen as such a sphinx, in many respects. The present title, however, does more justice to the topics discussed, and is more eloquent to an American public.

Como, Italy, December 2009

---

*Originally, *Una sfinge senza enigmi. Aspetti figure e momenti di vita, cultura e civiltà dagli Stati Uniti contemporanei*, prefazione di Sergio Romano (Firenze: Le Lettere 2001) pp. 164. I wish to thank Stephanie Bucci, Yvonne Robinson, Hannah Lubin, Lauren Skrabala, and Ashley Pony, who in different stages helped me translate this book from its original Italian, and edited it quite substantially for this English edition.

Aknowledgments

I want to thank the Office of Scholarly and Literary Publications of Georgetown University and its director, Dr. Carole Sargent, who supervised the editing of the English translation. My deepest thanks in particular go to the editors, Natalie Kimber and Alison Crowley, who did a wonderful job at polishing my English prose.

Paolo L. Bernardini

Introduction

The idea of writing about contemporary America goes back to my first stay in the United States, in the spring of 1992, in Baton Rouge, where I was a visiting scholar at Louisiana State University.

That stay, as well as all of my subsequent visits, including to Providence, where I worked on a research project on the Jewish presence in the Americas before the Modern Era (and on the presence of the Americas in Jewish consciousness and culture in Europe), proved to be all too brief. My research was too time-consuming, to allow me to examine aspects of contemporary America, which, though unrelated to my formal research, I would have liked to study and present to the Italian public—a public that usually, in all but rare exceptions, has only trite and partial perspectives on America, characterized by a propensity to stereotype, often by those who have never lived, or even set foot, in America.

The perspective is at times tainted by anti-Americanism, a chronic disease plaguing a particular segment of the Italian Left which is only now beginning to be overcome. On the other hand, there is the idealized vision of America, of great "space," "potential," and "innovation," a vision that led Jean Baudrillard to write an enigmatic book twenty years ago, which, without touching the peak of Baudrillard's thinking, dominates many of the Italian speculations on, and representations of, the New World. Such speculations often give way to "americanophile" movements and attitudes at times as superficial as those arising from the (declining) trend of "americanophobia".

Circumstances changed, for me, between 1998 and 1999. From the end of September 1998 to the end of July 1999, I was given an exceptional opportunity to write on, but first, to think about and see, contemporary America. As a member of the School of Historical Studies at the Institute for Advanced Study in Princeton, the perspective I gained could not have been more welcome.

The other fellows and the permanent faculty enriched my experience at that truly unique research center. It is simultaneously heir to the European humanistic tradition and pioneer in international scientific progress. It is open to innovation, such as theoretical biology, or Chinese culture and art, now a flourishing field in the United States. It is also conservative, if by conservative one means the just spirit that brings people and their institutions to conserve that which, based on personal conviction or widely accepted consensus, seems worthy of being preserved as something excellent and/or significant.

My research at the Institute, however, was not on contemporary American culture, but rather on the Italian Protestant jurist Alberico Gentili (1552-1608) and his 1584 unpublished treatise *De Papatu Romanu Antichristo*, a political and theological attack on the Catholic Church. These were clearly two different worlds. Thus, the problem: how could a historian of the Early Modern Era approach the study of contemporary America?

A possible answer came first in the example of one of the greatest intellectuals of our time, Albert O. Hirschman, who was the first to teach us to practice, with measure and method, periodic healthy self-subversions and regenerative spiritual baths, while maintaining at the same time one's identity as a scholar and as an ethical being. America at the close of the millennium is, of course, entirely different from Elizabethan England of Alberico Gentili's time. Therefore, it is quite remote from my usual area of focus, which is the eighteenth century. And differences in content often call for differences in form.

An eighteenth century scholar of importance such as Robert Darnton was able to give us a brilliant account of the fall of the Berlin Wall (*Berlin Journal 1989-1990*, New York, Norton 1991), having had the opportunity to live in the German capital during that fateful year. Thus he was also able to rediscover aspects of his youthful journalistic avocation as a crime reporter for the *New York Times*.

The twenty-six short essays that make up this American notebook consider many different aspects of contemporary American culture. I have imposed no precise structure. The goal here is to provide a fragmented vision, and a series of starting points for reflection on contemporary phenomena, without any specific interpretative end or approach in mind. The essays touch upon cinema, literature, museums, schools, presidents, and even Uncle Sam. Some aspects and phenomena—in the most general, Kantian sense of the word—are quite well known and accessible to the European public, for example, Stanley Kubrick's last film, *Eyes Wide Shut*; or the never-ending debate about Thomas Jefferson as a moral and political figure; or the intervention in Kosovo and how it was manipulated by the mass media.

Much less known, however, are some other aspects on which I focused—such as an exhibition in Colorado about the Native Americans massacred at Sand Creek, or the works and death of Texan poet Vassar Millar—some of which are unfamiliar to most Americans, and completely unknown to Europeans. Nevertheless these aspects deserve to be more widely known. While there is no overarching reason for the choice of the topics in each of the twenty-six essays, there is nonetheless a common intention, a common stylistic denominator. A young and bright contemporary historian, Timothy Garton Ash, author of a magnificent depiction of contemporary Eastern Europe with the revealing title *History of the Present* (London: Penguin Press, 1999), taught, or rather, reaffirmed the use of a sort of 'journalistic' style to treat present-day topics with a historical approach: sharp sentences, a sense of immediacy, and above all a declaration of intent that clearly indicates the subject, why it is being addressed, and what the author wants to express. The use of journalistic elements of style, therefore, would not be perceived as an affectation; rather, as an absolute necessity for clarity, better realism, and provocation. But in the end it is difficult to classify a collection of essays such as this. An American might see it as an attempt at "cultural history," maybe giving it too much credit. An Italian, on the other hand, might see it as an exercise in nonfiction art prose, following in the Italian tradition of the travelogue with the provocative use of two styles: the drawn-out and pleasant narrative (in the vein of Emilio Cecchi, Mario Praz, and Giorgio Manganelli), alternating with a more stringent articulation of the phrase. In any case, it is not so much the classification as a genre that counts, as it is the significance of the essays.

There is not, therefore, a precise design in the choice of topics, nor is there inherent logic to their order other than their division into four thematic areas, which are themselves quite loose:

I On African-Americans, Native Americans, and Jews (and more);
II On Men, Poets, and Presidents (and not only);
III On Knowledge and Understanding (men and places);
IV On Wars and Other Places (in peace).

One fundamental idea, however, informs the presentation of the material, and even earlier, in the decision to approach this material critically. The United States of America has become not only the most potent but also the only world power. The fall of the USSR, caused by the internal collapse of the socio-economic and political structures worn out by a century of imperialistic and dictatorial dominion, has been coupled with the creation of a political entity, the European Union, which is clearly in its infancy. Notwithstanding its daring monetary union, with the creation (perhaps too hasty) of a common currency, Europe as a political entity does not yet exist. There is no unified military—an extremely serious missing element—nor do the Parliament and the Commission work in the same way and with the same power as the Senate and Congress in the United States. And Japan, though showing some signs of recovery, cannot seem to dig itself out of the economic stagnation into which it has been sinking for several years.

In February 1992, as a visiting researcher at Louisiana State University, while driving around in my old Japanese car, I saw many billboards that showed the dollar bill, and encouraged the spending of it. The slogan was "Buck the Recession!" Since then the recession has been thoroughly halted, while the amount spent by Americans has increased (as have their earnings, obviously, even though Americans tend to spend more money than they actually have, a trend facilitated by the credit card system). The American car industry, thanks to a strong effort and aggressive investments, has surpassed the Japanese one, which was still dominant at the beginning of the 90s. Microsoft alone earns more than the three main American car manufacturers combined. It generates, if not for everyone, immense wealth. It hires, and it spends. The airplane that took my wife to a job interview in Seattle was literally full of young men and women heading to the pleasant state of Washington to be interviewed at Bill's mega-company. Some of them were shocked to learn that my wife Laura was interviewing for a relatively low-paying job at a little known university.

In 1992, at Louisiana State University, there lived a tall young black man, with a kind and placid air, a gentle giant. Shaquille O'Neal, who today is one of the most celebrated players in the NBA, was then just a student. Not even he could have imagined the multimillion-dollar salary he now earns, further increased by endorsements. The American economy has not simply grown in the past ten years; it has taken off. It is therefore worthwhile to look into some cultural aspects of the richest and most powerful country in the world. Not that one should approach it with celebratory aims: contemporary America is not the Athens of Pericles, nor the Florence of Lorenzo de' Medici or the Paris of Voltaire. And yet one ought not to approach it with purely negative opinions either, with the hope of coming to the conclusion that yes, Americans are rich and powerful, but that their cultural heritage (and their history) are decidedly inferior to Europe's. Both of these approaches are misguided, and influenced by opposite sides of the same prejudice or inferiority/superiority complex. The inquiring spirit serves first of all a phenomenological goal (not so much in the spirit of Husserl as in that of sociologists Georg Simmel or Siegfried Kracauer): to present material, often not well known because the tools and at times the desire to discover them are absent. The ultimate goal therefore, is to provide, even before the results of one's own reflection, which are inevitably present, material for future, autonomous research and reflection.

Given that this book is not the result of systematic research, the author feels in a way exempt from the often difficult task of drawing some overarching conclusion, and of neatly tying together the various lines of thought, in order to justify, in retrospect, the entire work. And yet, some extemporaneous notes of this kind arise from the reconsideration of the material itself. Standing alone at the summit of global wealth, America is and remains inescapably linked to its relationships with the rest of the world, even if many

Americans would rather do without them. The point of comparison is still Europe, but this position is becoming increasingly unstable. Some now look for different bases of comparison: Africa, for example, from which the first slaves embarked, or Latin America (which, however, goes back to European culture, given its strong Spanish and Portuguese heritage), from which America gets its greatest number of immigrants. On the one hand, there is a tightening of the WASP culture, still very strong today, and on the other hand, there is a true opening up to the multicultural world by the middle class. This, in many cases, makes America a truly successful melting pot, much more successful than in the past, and at various socio-economic levels.

As for public and individual morality, there has arisen a much more jaded consciousness among Americans than in the past. The Clinton scandal did maintain the media's attention, but it seemed to me more a way of passing time than a topic of real interest. The oscillations of the Dow-Jones seem to capture more sustained public interest, as do the results of important football, basketball, and baseball games. Another event that captivated the interest of Americans occurred just before I left the United States: the premature death of John F. Kennedy, Jr., with his beautiful wife and her sister during a night flight over the waters off of Martha's Vineyard; waters so American, so linked to the Kennedys that they were practically their family's swimming pool.

This Kennedy tragedy shook America far more deeply than did the sexual exploits of the plump Monica Lewinsky in the crowded hallways of the White House. Unexpected death, *mors improvisa* the most feared kind of death in medieval as well as modern Christian Europe, is far more disturbing and striking than a sex scandal. And it brings us back to the inescapable: no matter how rich, how happy, or even simply how sated we are, none of us can escape death. We can't avoid destiny. Hence the quasi-mystical, quasi-metaphysical pages that accompanied reports of the incident, as well as the postmodern funeral, complete with ashes spread over the ocean from a military ship, no photographs allowed, no public event, full of "understatement." Yet, at the same time, it was the exact opposite of "understatement," something in the genes, as well as in the destiny, of the Kennedys.

Today's America is shaken by menacing clouds on the horizon, the nature of which is unclear. Will there be a recession? Will India and Pakistan start a nuclear war? Will the drift of the African continent and the semi-drift of the South American subcontinent change the course of our well-being? What type of entity is, in fact, the European Union? We see an America that contemplates above all its own past, and Europe's past, in order to celebrate, perhaps, its own triumphs, but also to shed light on those shady areas of its conscience. Hence we witness the creation of new museums, memorials, and more and more publications of historical books.

This American notebook wishes to provide an account of these things and others, just a few stars from the American galaxy. The account has its limitations, and is deliberately impressionist (in the manner of Jules Lemâitre, an unsurpassed master essayist), while at the same time trying its best to achieve an objective view.

Padova, Italy, March 2001.

I

On African Americans, Native Americans, and Jews (and more)

These first six chapters offer portraits of minorities, or rather, cultural and intellectual events relating to minorities, as I experienced them in 1998-1999. These include African Americans in a major scholarly contribution to oral history, by Ira Berlin and Steve Miller; Native Americans in a Colorado exhibit devoted to the Sand Creek massacre; the Jews of New York and their claims to "aristocracy;" refugees to America as represented in a photo exhibition at the New York Historical Society; the representation of the Shoah in the recently inaugurated Battery Park Museum of the Holocaust; and finally the Hutterites, a Protestant sect that fled to the American colonies and now is still present in the USA. I wrote this last chapter thanks to my direct encounter with Jon and Claudia Swan. Jon is a journalist who amply wrote about the Hutterites as a "community experiment" at the time of various 1968 quests for Utopia.

If the USA is a melting pot, the soup in the pot does not stop boiling for even a single minute. The numerous components of the American society are constantly making justified claims to be heard; and if they do not make those claims by themselves, intellectuals and public figures fight their fight for them. Only by understanding several components of American society on the eve of the year 2000 can we understand the reaction of the entire American society to the post-2000 events. At the time I wrote these essays in 1998-1999 the USA seemed in a sort of perfect equilibrium. Probably, however, it was not so perfect, and a decade of crisis followed. Although I am far from endorsing his liberal agenda, I cannot fail to note that an African American is now President of the USA. Before Obama, this happened only (or rather, was anticipated only) in movies. This event sheds a peculiar light on the first essay.

1

African-American Destinies

The endless discourse on discrimination and racism in the United States

Before a new book by historians Ira Berlin and Steve Miller was even published, it was discussed among intellectuals and publicized in major journals. There were even clandestine copies of the abstract in circulation. The book, *Remembering Slavery: African Americans Talk About Their Experiences of Slavery and Freedom,* is a collection of dozens of meticulously transcribed interviews with ex-slaves who were young during the Civil War. The subsequent eradication of slavery was like a gust of wind bringing fresh air to the sunny, arid, bloodstained states of the South.

These men and women, elderly but with memories of servitude still engraved like indelible wounds causing agony at the gentlest touch, were interviewed by aspiring historians, often unemployed college graduates. This was during the 1930s, at the height of the Depression, when the dust from the wreckage of Wall Street still flooded the streets and the souls of America. The government was busy finding new ways to employ the masses of unemployed, cultured, young and not-so-young adults. The Federal Writers' Project was one such way. The new science of anthropology was flourishing with intellectuals like Radin and Boas, and someone suggested employing all those penniless white-collars to conduct oral history experiments. There was an abundance of ex-slaves, and with the aid of the latest technology in audio recording, one could conduct interviews about their life in the Deep South during the time when they were deprived of legal rights and still essentially the property of the landowners. In this way, it was possible to preserve particular moments in history that were otherwise destined to be forgotten: most of the ex-slaves were illiterate and few among the literate would have considered leaving memoirs. The aim of recording these histories, therefore, was to provide a scientific foundation and a vision of a world that went beyond the stereotypical, though somewhat truthful, Uncle Tom. These interviews, dozens of reels of tape, were never published, but they were preserved in various archives in Texas and Washington, D.C.

Ira Berlin, professor of African-American history at the University of Maryland, unearthed the reels years ago. Berlin sustains, and it is difficult to contradict him, that "slavery is as much a part of the history of white America as the history of black America." And so it is. And so Americans will once again be confronted by the brutality of their past.

Readers will discover, for instance, one harsh punishment for stealing candy. Henrietta, a little girl from West Point, Virginia, painfully recalled that while she was being whipped, her master shoved her face under the seat of a rocking chair, leaving her face disfigured for life. Other interviews recount stories of rape and massacre. However, there are also stories of moral and physical resistance, of adventurous escapes, of courage and sensitivity. Perhaps these testimonies do not shed new light; nonetheless, the force of direct narration will certainly contribute to the dissipation of fog in our consciousness and thereby in our judgments.

Another book published in 1998 reminds Americans that the passage from slavery to emancipation is complex and is perhaps still taking place. The book discusses the change of traditional discrimination patterns between black minorities and white majorities, maintaining that it may not be as simple as the elimination of old laws and the creation of new ones. The autobiography is titled *Walking with the Wind*, and a literal translation into Italian would betray the essence of its meaning. In Italy, a country where Machiavellian concepts are part of *la vita quotidiana*, to "go with the wind" would suggest opportunistic behavior. The title is, however, a romantic one; not in the sappy Scarlett O'Hara sense but in the virile and suffered sense, because "wind" is a metaphor for civil protest against discrimination. The book is by an African-American congressman, John Lewis.

Lewis, approaching sixty years of age and a man of great accomplishment, is known throughout the country and the world as one of the leading civil rights proponents. Congressman Lewis recently spoke in Providence, Rhode Island. He wore an impeccable blue suit and spoke with a deep voice. With an acute yet pensive expression, he enthralled the crowd of both blacks and whites in the small Sheldon Street Church. *Walking with the Wind* narrates the story of an uncommonly curious young boy raised in a small farming town in Alabama. One day during the difficult post-war period he went to the city of Troy to borrow books from the local public library. He was refused the privilege because he was a "nigger," and therefore, according to the white folks, his interests should lay elsewhere. Subsequently, Lewis started to follow anti-segregationist movements. He began to read Gandhi, like many others, in particular his friend and comrade Martin Luther King, Jr. John Lewis started a long series of campaigns, of sit-ins, of political demonstrations. He did not receive an equally peaceful response from the authorities. Instead, he was frequently beaten and clubbed.

Today, his elegant baldness is in contrast to those early days when policemen habitually threw lighted cigarettes in his full, curly black hair. Lewis was present on Bloody Sunday in torrid Selma, in his Alabama, when the police loaded and shot into a crowd of nonviolent demonstrators. In 1953, still a very young man, he was at Martin Luther King's side at the Lincoln Memorial, protesting against discrimination in front of 200,000 people, arousing enthusiasm in all. It was that very occasion in which King delivered his "I Have a Dream" speech. John F. Kennedy admired the young Lewis and more than once he observed that the fire that ignites him wouldn't die.

In the meantime, Martin Luther King and John Kennedy have both been killed. Lewis continues the battle. From the benches of Congress he defends the civil rights of African Americans. Much has changed since that bloody day in Selma. Much has been ameliorated. There are no longer odiously racist governors like George Wallace, and discriminatory laws have been abolished. And yet, as Lewis himself admits, the struggle for integration is not finished, nor can it be, for now "racism is perhaps more invisible." Even President Clinton sparked a national debate regarding the reconciliation of racial differences when he observed that there are many organizations and individuals who with great subtlety continue to propagate racist ideals. Just like Lewis, America still has a long road ahead. The idea that racism has become invisible does not mean that it has disappeared. Lewis offers us testimony to a long, perhaps endless militancy. The wind that carries him, the wind of civil rights, of non-violent protest, and denouncement of discrimination, continues to blow.

2

The Lost Footprints of Sand Creek

The Colorado History Museum in Denver evokes the Sand Creek Massacre: one of the most tragic events in American history

The third arrow, look for it at the bottom of Sand Creek...

This verse, sung by the Italian singer-songwriter Fabrizio de André, was composed in remembrance of the misfortunes of Native Americans. At dawn on November 29, 1864, seven hundred volunteer soldiers led by Colonel John M. Chivington, already a Civil War hero, wrought havoc upon the mile-long bend of the Sandy Creek River where Cheyenne Chief Black Kettle and his allies the Arapaho had established their base camp. At the time of the assault neither the Chief nor his men were at the camp. They had all gone hunting. All that remained in the camp were the elderly, women, children, and livestock. A white flag billowed high above a tent next to the stars and stripes of the Union. Like Byron's Assyrian king, the young American soldiers raged upon those helpless Native Americans like a pack of wolves. Not encountering any resistance, in several hours they killed a hundred and fifty innocent people and raped the women. The children who had fled to the river were hunted down and mutilated, their *membra disiecta* displayed like trophies.

The Civil War was not yet over when these volunteers in torrid Colorado waged war against the Cheyenne, who were obstinate, astute, perhaps even cruel, but no more so than any side in the war. Black Kettle, a wise leader, had proposed a truce, and in Washington there was equally ardent hope for an end to the hostilities. The massacre at Sand Creek could have been easily avoided, and is inexplicable for this very reason.

Three years after the tragedy motives for the hostility of Colonel Chivington, whom Congress described as a butcher, finally came to light. Three years prior to the massacre, his then-seventeen-year-old daughter was raped by some Cheyenne in western Colorado. With that, the fate of the Methodist pastor-turned-intrepid-soldier and methodical persecutor of Indians was decided.

At times, the American quest for remembrance follows a predictable pattern. It is therefore no surprise that during the late '60s and the early '70s the events of Sand Creek resurfaced in the American consciousness and were subsequently recounted to the rest of the world. The discussions and descriptions of the tragedy were, both in the media and at the cinema, intended as indirect criticism of American initiatives in Vietnam. The horrific attack set a shameful historical precedent for the equally vile 1969 Marine attack on the Vietnamese village of My Lai. Although a century had elapsed between the two episodes, just as at Sand Creek, at My Lai hundreds of innocent women, children and elderly perished under American fire. The savage brutality of modern warfare left the Cheyenne defenseless. Their mortality was reduced to one final and sacred gesture. As they symbolically pointed their bows to the sky and launched their arrows into the sun's rays, which crudely illuminated their fatal destinies, a curse was cast against their assailants.

Theodore V. Olsen's novel *Arrow in the Sun*, published in 1970, recounts the Sand Creek Massacre. In the same year the director Ralph Nelson, known for his human rights and environmental activism, produced a film titled *Soldier Blue* based on Olsen's book. Due to the film's success the book was subsequently reprinted the following year under the title of the film. Nelson considered Sand Creek the perfect metaphorical portent to underline the atrocities of the current "dirty war." While his timing was auspicious, the film met with more success in Europe than in the U.S. The film's last rapid, crude scenes depict with grisly detail the massacre and an attempt to flee by the two protagonists, a splendid Peter Strauss and a passionate Candice Bergen. Perhaps today, more than the film or the book, one remembers the musical score written by Buffy Sainte Marie, a Native American who wrote *Up Where We Belong*, a pleasant melody still heard more than thirty years later.

America as a whole seems to have forgotten Vietnam as Europe has forgotten *Soldier Blue*. And yet, prosperous America, in a desperate search for values that go beyond the Dow Jones and the Super Bowl, is beginning to question its past. In Denver, there is an exhibition, or rather a memoriam, of the massacre at Sand Creek. Also on display are Spencers, the first semi-automatic rifles that were also used during the Civil War, along with Native American crafts, bow and arrows, illustrations, paintings, and old maps. Videotaped interviews with survivors' descendents are projected on the walls. There also hangs a huge American flag bearing fewer stars than today, tainted gray by the error of that bloody autumn day.

The massacre goes beyond the walls of the exposition in Denver. In 1999, while America examined its conscience about its past, just one Native American sat in Congress, Ben Nighthorse Campbell. Campbell believes that Sand Creek was one of the most devastating and shameful episodes in American history. He is from Colorado, where the few remaining Native Americans keep the memory of the massacre alive. A team of archaeologists is currently excavating to find the exact location where the massacre took place, for Sand Creek is the only major battle site—if one chooses to call it a battle rather than a slaughter—that archaeologists are unable to locate. Identifying where the massacre took place is a necessary first step for Congressman Campbell as well as for Congress. The second step is creation of a memorial honoring the lives of the Indians who were slaughtered. Paying homage to the Indians of Sand Creek will help to always keep the violent and destructive nature of war alive in the American conscience. Paradoxically, Colorado already has a town named Chivington, in memory of the Colonel. Yet, the place where he carried out his senseless vendetta has yet to be found. Without doubt, American efficiency and sophisticated technology will bring to the surface the bows and arrows about which De André and Buffy Sainte Marie, as well as many others, sang. However, notwithstanding the amount of time that has passed, the wounds of that bloody and wretched episode will never completely heal.

3

Bad Blue Blood: New York Jewish Aristocracy

The Jewish-American community's incredible vitality preserves fading European traditions

In New York City some restaurants require reservations several months in advance, not necessarily because these trendy Asian or European 'new cuisine' hotspots prepare exquisite entrees, but more important, because they offer exclusive wine lists and elegant settings. For those who partake, this is more than merely fine dining: it is a sign of success. The combination of exclusive wine, an elegant setting and a select crowd creates a sophisticated ambiance and an unforgettable dining experience, albeit one somewhat disrupted by over-obsessive waiters who stand at your back ready to whisk away even the tiniest speck that falls upon your table. Jack Freiberg, a native New Yorker and art historian whose heart is torn between Rome's fountains and the Big Apple's skyline, notes that on Yom Kippur those restaurants are deserted. No one of fashion will enter, for without the usual clientele the ambiance loses all its glamour and no one wants to throw away a couple of hundred dollars not to be seen.

New York City is home to the largest metropolitan Jewish community in the world. Beyond the canonical subdivision of Orthodox, Conservative and Reform, the New Jerusalem on the Hudson is home to every different Jewish sect. When Ismar Schorsch, president of the Jewish Theological Seminary, the backbone of Jewish-American academic conservatism, confessed to the *New York Times* that he was disappointed and disturbed by Clinton's behavior, many feared that his comments would catapult the incorrigible seducer right out of office.

The New York Jewish community is more than a small world. It is a universe of inexhaustible fascination where unforgettable experiences of life, death, religion and thought take place. That which the Nazi hurricane swept away in Europe thereby denying the Old Continent of some of its most profound cultural traditions is conserved here, unaltered, and at the same time, modified by the new world for better integration. In Brooklyn, a recent marriage of unusual pomp between two young members of the Hasidim sect reveals this duality. Brooklyn is unique, for nowhere else in the world do so many diverse ethnicities and nationalities reside together. Among these are Italians who have made *Broccolino* their historical stomping ground as well as their point of departure for far more noble adventures on the island of Manhattan. They cross that eponymous bridge as if they were embarking upon a voyage of discovery and fortune. Notwithstanding their radical differences, Jews and Italians have lived together in Brooklyn without the usual interracial friction for a long time. Director Robert De Niro pointed out that the same cannot be said of relationships between Italians and African Americans, or African Americans and Jews.

The Hasidim, whose name means "pious" or "devout," belong to a sect that originated in Eastern Europe at the beginning of the eighteenth century. It developed after an anguished period in European Jewish history which witnessed the new, false messiah Sabbatai Zevi and the massacres of Chmielmicki in Poland. The Pious, animated by a doctrine similar to mysticism and joined by a tight fraternal community, spread throughout all of Central Eastern Europe inspired by the teachings of Israel ben Eliezer. Each individual group followed the teachings of one of the disciples of ben Eliezer, spreading the message from one disciple to another. These spiritual leaders were called *Zaddikim*, "the righteous ones." According to the Talmud, these thirty-six "righteous ones" peacefully sustained the world by administrating justice. They became a true aristocratic caste within the sect, often living in great opulence, revered and honored like Sultans. Unlike Sultans, however, they were obligated to abstain from polygamy, as their laws prohibited it.

Notwithstanding the Holocaust, the Hasidim still persevere. From the cold oriental plains, from the Lithuanian, Moravian and Baltic villages, and from the peaceful, melancholic shores of the

Danube or the Oder, their stories pass to the Manhattan skyscrapers where the sky is not covered by majestic storks and other migrating birds, but by swarms of helicopters that frenetically load and unload businessmen and tourists. And in Brooklyn, the Hasidim celebrate a special wedding between two of their young, belonging to two of the most ancient families of the sect whose genealogy can be traced back to the epoch of Eliezer, and perhaps earlier. The entire community celebrates in completely black attire consisting of a hat with long flaps and a beard with long dark braids. But this time the men's profiles inspire hope and cheerfulness. The community Zaddik, who is no longer called Zaddik but instead *Rebbe*, and who no longer adopts the rituals of his predecessors, insists that the wedding be truly aristocratic. The heirs, whom everyone anxiously awaits, will represent the best of the Hasidim -- not an aristocracy of wealth, for generally they are not affluent, but rather, of bloodline.

We confront a peculiar destiny. The Jews, historically denied noble status, have constructed their own. It originates in that distant and violent Poland where, at the dawn of the eighteenth century, aristocrats were their nemesis. In reality, the Jews have simply reclaimed the political system of the ancient Jewish state wherein nobility always existed. After the fall of the Second Temple, history determined otherwise. That same Jew who at one time was noble was forever branded as having "bad blood." This was true in Spain under Ferdinand and Isabel and throughout anti-Semitic, Darwinian and racist Europe at the end of the nineteenth century. The concept of bad blood inspired the Holy Office's condemnations just like the Romantic age's praise of evil, the impure, the irregular, and vice. Wrote Arthur Rimbaud, inspiring French director Leo Carax, in his *Mauvais sang* one of the poems in *Une Saison en Enfer*: "Marching, burdens, the desert, boredom and anger."

And yet, America is great because it transforms, *ex novo*, "bad blood" into "blue blood." Even if such a transformation for this festive group of men with long braids and long black flaps is a mere illusion, there is nonetheless the suggestion of redemption in all this. Perhaps all nobility is based upon an illusion. To believe this illusion is not as pernicious as to believe the many other illusions of nobility.

As the crowd fervently moves amongst the red bricks and elegant streets which are neatly lined with trees and in a vague way evoke the finer London quarters, this gigantic Brooklyn neighborhood looks upon Manhattan from the other side of the river with neither envy nor inferiority.

4

The Road to Refuge

An exhibition of photographs depicting political refugees in the United States at the New York Historical Society

The setting is solemn.

The New York Historical Society is located in Central Park West, in an imposing neoclassical building at the end of 77th Street. Across the street, Central Park is immersed in the summer heat, and in front is the Museum of Natural History. Groups of students scurry around the great museum, at the time hosting an exhibition on infectious diseases in history. Nearby, silent and discreet, safeguarded by an uncompromising doorman usually of Indian or Spanish nationality, are some of the most splendid mansions belonging to Manhattan's most prominent elite.

From one of the buildings of questionable architectural value, a supermodel in trendy workout gear stalks into Central Park like a metropolitan leopard. Meanwhile, a flamboyantly dressed elderly lady, assiduously accompanied by her court of small dogs, also -- for different reasons than the model -- swiftly heads for the grassy recesses and the sheltered clearings of the park.

In the smoldering heat of July 1999, the New York Historical Society hosted an insightful exhibition of photographs from the lives of political refugees in the United States. The setting was mostly New York: not only the city and its suburbs ranging from Long Island to Hempstead, but also upstate New York, traditionally hospitable to political refugees from all over the world. The artist was Mel Rosenthal, a renowned photographer and university professor, and as one would guess from his name, son of Russian Jewish immigrants. It was clear from the outset that there was more than a superficial understanding between photographer and subject. The series of remarkable black-and-white images begun in the mid 1980s documented an extraordinary universe.

The United States has traditionally welcomed political refugees from many different countries. They are more or less legally entitled to refugee status, and the US has practically no viable solution for their continual influx. Rosenthal enthusiastically describes a range of possible alternatives for these numerous nationalities and ethnicities that converge in the American "melting pot," adding these to the increasing cultural nuances that characterize the U.S. From the photographed subjects' origins to the fragmented, uncertain, and often strenuous flow of daily life, Rosenthal subtly recreates *per speculum* the course of modern history. The awareness he inspires of present day wars and despotic regimes that continue to force people to immigrate, or to seek political refuge, is staggering. However, dictatorships and ethnic cleansing are not the only factors that force open the sealed iron gates to the road of refuge. Most often, the necessity to flee the misery of famine and the desire for a better future, or, at least, the hope for a better future for oneself and one's family, is more than sufficient.

Although Rosenthal prefers to concentrate on the life of political refugees, he recognizes that the distinction between an immigrant and a political refugee is a subtle one. Beyond the categorical distinctions imposed by international law, there are no fundamental differences in the struggle for survival between refugees and immigrants for whom the flight from misery is, in effect, the flight from dictatorship. Often, African and Asian countries—Indonesia being a prime example—have been reduced to famine due to the indulgences of a dictator. In cases like these, accepting refugees also serves (given the past complications with regimes like Suharto's) to liberate one's conscience as if to pay off a debt. A country is rarely, in fact almost never, destined to absolute poverty due to the mere absence of natural resources.

Rosenthal opens with simple frames where the least amount of subject posing blends perfectly with his natural narration style. This technique allows him to directly and perfectly portray micro-worlds while condensing the habits, languages, customs, and clothing of the macro-worlds that pulsate from the suburban valleys, hills and mountains of upstate New York, where swarms of thriving and industrious immigrants, drawn and vitalized by that lower barycenter (the inexhaustible Big Apple in its constant state of expansion), are guided by American economic power.

Profiles, behaviors, gazes and accents radically change from one community to the next, yet the fundamental dialectic that animates the life of all refugees is, in the end, one and the same. Conciliation, or its opposite, laceration, is between one's ethno-cultural and religious identity and the necessity to earn one's existence within a system that is equally as promising as it is merciless and rigid. That system is obviously the North American labor (and thus life-giving) market. Rosenthal, with the perspective of one who understands because he himself has lived it, captures that instant of tension created by the juxtaposition of these exigencies which are contradictory and yet complementary. For this reason his images are reconciling, and often they are splendidly reconciled. A son of the South Bronx, once the neighborhood of the respectable European bourgeois and presently an urban ghetto, Rosenthal transmits noteworthy emotions through his photographs: he works in fragments, a kaleidoscope of profiles and situations.

Even for those who live in the multi-ethnicity of New York, where what is elsewhere considered "eccentric" is normal, these wrinkled, enigmatic, feline profiles provoke emotional reactions. Ironically, their infinite humaneness seems nonhuman. Among women taking a walk in suburban Liverpool we see refugees from Laos, allies of the United States during the Vietnam War, who were harshly oppressed from the moment in which the communist regime claimed victory. A Cambodian family bears the same stigmata of suffering. A grayed father recounts, didactically, when huge airplanes circled over his country and dropped bombs in every direction, forcing them to abandon their homes and country. In these cases and many others, the United States has a certain degree of responsibility: a dirty conscience that it can wipe clean only by accepting these populations without creating unnecessary obstacles. More recent cases of political refugees also exist. Bosnian families are living testimony of populations that are perennially subjected to flight, extermination, and international discord. Similarly, there are Kurdish families who, notwithstanding their anguish and upheaval, are cheerful in their impoverished Johnson City suburb.

The most striking feature of Rosenthal's work above all in the younger generations he portrays (at times going to the extreme of risking his life as when he attempted to photograph some adolescent members of a Vietnamese gang), is the immigrants' passionate attempts to remain faithful to their ethnic and religious identities, displaying their determination not to allow their origins to be eclipsed by the New World's environment. Tibetan Buddhist Monks are represented at the height of their function and, when possible, at their reconstructed temples in the Bronx and in Brooklyn. Russian Jews, naturally a subject close to Rosenthal, are captured in their moment of return to Judaism: a spectacular blond baby sitting in a bare classroom with just a blackboard on which a few words from the sacred language are written. In DeWitt, a Russian immigrant carries the Torah Scroll with great solemnity and attention.

Through these photos one learns much about the tormented world from which these refugees fled. The manifold uncertainty during the breakup of the Soviet Union caused a fierce revival of anti-Semitism. The consequences were more practical and violent than theoretical, for it prevented many Jews from freely practicing their religion. The media, particularly in Europe, practically ignored this fact, along with other equally serious problems; American media is naturally much more attentive to these phenomena. Rosenthal also included the recently formed ethnic mix of Amerasians: children of American soldiers and Vietnamese women, conceived during the drawn out American misadventure in the Far East. These children, from an anthropological point of view, create a unique community, for they are half American yet often face discrimination and are rarely accepted into mainstream America. From the Old World— Latvia, Lithuania, and Russia—artists and musicians often arrive and, thanks to their professions, are able to integrate into schools and orchestras. Consider however the Ethiopian doctors whose medical degrees are not recognized; thus their only alternative is to work as nurses. On the same note, we see Afghan attorneys who drive taxis or Pakistani university professors who find employment in factories.

The road to refuge can be incredibly harsh. The whole United

States, and in particular New York, has always served as a landing dock for political refugees and immigrants from around the world. For this reason, across America many towns are baptized with names recalling a particular place of origin, paying homage to those who were persecuted there for either religious or political reasons. For example, New Paltz, the new Palatine, refers to the strip of land between Germany and France where the highest concentration of Protestants in modern history were persecuted. Or, perhaps, a town's baptismal name evokes, in the new American empire, the great empires of the past: Athens, Rome, Syracuse. In fact, Syracuse, a university town, hosts one of the largest refugee communities in the state. Rosenthal, inasmuch as he aims for objectivity, tends at times to give preference to sentimental undertones that characterize the life of a political refugee, often metaphorically referred to as the valley of tears.

An example of this approach is his delicate photograph of a little Palestinian girl wrapped in traditional light-colored clothing, turning and braking on her roller blades in front of her father's electronics shop in Bay Ridge, Brooklyn. Her gaze communicates an inner calmness, an innate trust for what her future holds. Such trust is not borne of the prideful-yet-somewhat-suffering expression of her father in the next photograph. The young are those who, as is natural, face with greater security and at times greater audacity, the road to refuge. Traditionally, the oldest usually sit around and chat endlessly in their mother tongue, revealing a certain disdain for the "American" language. A provocative and rather telling image is that of two Russian immigrants with melancholic expressions playing a game of chess at Brighton Beach.

Exiting the neoclassical building and emerging into the July haze, one looks differently upon the Indian, Pakistani, and Vietnamese doormen standing at the entrances of the buildings that belong to those New York magnates. While it is easy to imagine Caucasians exiting from those entrances, it is less easy to imagine them standing in front and working as doormen, but this is part of the game. Only those immigrants who belong to families dating back several generations have been able to successfully integrate themselves into American society: a society created by immigrants. Thus, the true distinguishing factor is seniority, for it does not necessarily matter whence one arrived but when one arrived. The American WASP maintains his status at the summit of economic well-being, while the Italians, Irish, Scottish, and others run a close second.

The Rosenthal exhibition, which often deviates from the theme by depicting simple immigrants and not only political refugees, can boast, among its many merits (which go beyond the technical and artistic ones), the immediacy of its images. The result is a superb and profound documentation of the heart and soul of America. Willingly and unwillingly, America is the only truly multi-ethnic country in the world. It welcomes daily into its immense space Africans and Asians who flee from hardship and persecution, as well as Europeans: Serbs, Bosnians, and Montenegrins.

It may be true what the Italian poet Eugenio Montale, Nobel laureate for literature in 1975, wrote: *"Your happiness walks on the edge of a razor blade."* The circumstances of political refugees and immigrants in general are precarious even when economic well-being, and thus a sense of stability, seems solidly achieved. And as the 1998 Amnesty International Report demonstrated, those who seek political asylum in the United States are at times subjected to preventative measures, such as time in prison without even committing a crime. Some sentences are for years.

In the end, these photographs communicate an almost complete sense of serenity, epitomized by the smiling and peaceful yet slightly melancholic profile of an elderly Czech actor. With a long white beard and a cylinder shaped berretta of the same color, he gazes upon Manhattan miming a proud military salute.

Walking along the frenetic and multi-colored streets of Brooklyn and Manhattan, one easily understands how much the world depicted through Rosenthal's photographs constitutes an infinitesimal but representative fragment of a society, open to the world and composed of all its nations and races.

5

The Holocaust at Battery Park

Reflections on New York's Holocaust Museum and the worldwide "Holocaust industry"

Seen from a distance, from the ferries departing for Ellis Island, it appears a bizarre Oriental pagoda, a gray mass extending across the furthermost point of opulent and pulsating Manhattan. Notwithstanding its 10,000 square meters of exposition space, the Museum of Jewish Heritage is not an imposing building; it is elevated several tens of meters or so above the murky water at Battery Park, composed of essentially three hexagonal floors, each slightly smaller than the one below, giving the impression of an awkward pagoda or the spires of a skyscraper somehow sawed off from the main tower and placed in an artificial and meager greenery, in fact like that of Battery Park. Legend has it that this park is where the first Jewish immigrants landed in distant 1645, when it was tolerant New Amsterdam. Arriving from South America, they were the first Jews to touch ground on North American soil.

The hexagonal form, according to director David Altshuler, recalls the six million deaths of the Holocaust. It should be specified, the six million *Jews* who died—if one wanted to architecturally render the total number of deaths, several more sides would need to be added. After years of planning and fundraising, the museum opened its doors in 1997. It now attracts tens of thousands of visitors, above all students many of whom are ignorant not only of the Holocaust, but also of almost every aspect of Jewish history pre- or post-Auschwitz.

Elie Wiesel, a great Jewish figure, New Yorker by adoption and recipient of the Nobel Peace Prize, greeted the museum enthusiastically: "I am deeply convinced that, besides the Yad Vashem in Israel, this museum can well become the most important, the most representative custodian of Jewish memory in the world." With a view overlooking the Statue of Liberty and with the support of the Jewish and non-Jewish intellectual elite of New York—politicians such as Mario Cuomo, Edward Koch, and George E. Pataki—such a wish should have been obtainable. But until now it had not occurred.

The tripartite structure of the building represents a rather traditional model, from Buddhism to Hegel, of a simple and simplistic language: Before, During, After. The Museum of Jewish Heritage, unfortunately, is greatly lacking on the Before. Thousands of years of Jewish history are entirely ignored; *tant bien que mal* for those who to some extent already know it, but not for those school groups or for the average American who, if not Jewish, traditionally overlook such history. This is not due solely to the shortcomings of elementary and secondary education. The first floor is dedicated entirely to the European and American Jewish experience dating from the second half of the nineteenth century; however, the European Jewish tradition dates back to at least 70 A.D. Except for those pioneers who reached America during the Colonial period (estimates place their numbers at about 2,000 at the dawn of the American Revolution), the Jewish American tradition dates back to the second half of the nineteenth century, to one period in particular arising from the immense waves of immigration to the New World, which characterize Central-Eastern Europe between Sedan and the First World War.

Up until this point, there are scarce facts or images, and the documents are of no major importance. Information is schematic but effective. In the first room, on the first floor, a multimedia apparatus projects various Jewish and Gentile images, along with not-very-well-articulated sounds. These include a *Kaddish* (funeral song) and biblical passages recounted in Yiddish, where, if you pause, it seems as if some type of psychedelic experience or a series of TV commercials of rapid sequence rose from within it. Until you get a headache or you realize that you are observing the same images over and over, the didactic itinerary appears coherent, even if it is difficult to reconsider in these few rooms the course of the European Diaspora at the end of the nineteenth century and the incipit of the twentieth century with its confusing, fragmented and limitless richness.

But, alas, the anabasis on the second floor suddenly brings us into another world, in an utterly different context, with hardly any reference to the first. In one moment the wall texts explain who the Jews are and what anti-Semitism is, and the next, in a single leap, feature tortures and mass exterminations. It would have been good to pay greater attention to the phenomena of anti-Semitism during the nineteenth century, (which was diligently studied in the U.S. by George L. Mosse, who passed away in 1999), above all in order to establish a link between the tragic events of 1933-1945 that appear -- inasmuch as they finally can -- completely unrelated to the reality of nineteenth century Europe. The second floor is called "The War against the Jews," a title which echoes to point of debate a well-known book. That book takes its title from Goebbels' noted statement to an assembly of Nazis before one extermination, "With sad announcement of future damage," as if he were a sort of dismal imitator of Dante's unforgettable harpies.

Here lies the dark soul of the museum.

In the descriptions and documentation of the by-now-well-known horrors, which are nevertheless always appalling, the New York museum almost competes with the grandiose, gloomy and ghastly Holocaust Memorial Museum in Washington, from which it drew its inspiration. There are spaces that document smaller and lesser-known episodes such as the *Saint Louis* that set sail from Hamburg to Cuba in 1939 on a catastrophic voyage of hope. The necessity to return to its homeland led to the consequential extermination of all the Jews who had unluckily boarded.

Also striking is the section dedicated to the children of the Holocaust, or the one about the camp at Theresienstadt where the regime simulated a peaceful and industrious Jewish community that co-existed with the surrounding community when, in reality, it was a concentration camp like all the others. And like the others, it had its tortures, deprivations, and exterminations. This is a reality virtually unknown despite the quantity of information we have today about those atrocious years.

Finally, as if awakened from a nightmare, heading toward the third floor, we ascend to the paradise of the reconstruction and the rebirth of the Israeli people, with necessary attention paid to American reality and obviously to Israeli reality. And here, through one of the windowed walls of the hexagon, is a view dominated by the ocean and the Statue of Liberty. Here one takes a deep breath of liberation for having survived the nightmare—a nightmare that conceivably speaks with different words but which is equally profound to the American, European, and worldwide consciousness. The explicative and didactic value, possibly somewhat exaggerated with respect to the presumed maturity of the American youth, is undeniable. How will those students react to learning how a gas mask works? Thinking of those who were thrown alive into cremation furnaces?

A black teacher asks a group of black students, "Do you know what a ghetto is?" A little girl, seven or eight years of age, responds, "Yes, it is a bad thing." Hers is a response that implies a certain awareness of the thing (and perhaps she has even heard conversations at home about "black ghettos," a reality familiar to Americans). There seem to be no Jews amongst the stream of visitors, mostly youth groups. A middle-aged women cries as she watches a video on deportation while simultaneously listening to a separate narration by an old woman projected on one of the many screens situated throughout the three-story building.

The use of multimedia, the disposition of the rooms, and the corridors and the illumination are all monuments to American museum technology, which hopefully will be replicated in Europe. There are also some objects of particular significance: the microscopic edition of the *Song of Songs*, with its dimensions of a gigantic stamp testifying to the most unexpected forms of attachment, despaired and despairing for all forms of tradition when threatened with one's own life. And there are documented important aspects about anti-Semitism during the Nazi regime, which are not always well known, such as Lithuanian anti-Semitism. The audio guides are in Meryl Streep's measured and touching voice.

It is legitimate, however, to ask: In an edifice with a name as promising as the Museum of Jewish Heritage, why is this heritage condensed into so few rooms, especially if it dates back over millennia? And why does the museum document the near-annihilation of this civilization and its heritage when it was not perfectly achieved? It would have been better to name it "Museum of Jewish Extermination," with all of the agonizing passivity—although it is a proud populace that knew how to survive the extermination first morally then physically—inherent in the adjective "Jewish." Maybe a museum recalling all of the exterminations of the century that have just ended -- the European and Asian ones, the African ones, more recently the Bosnian and Serbian ones, and, *in primis*, the Armenian ones -- would be of greater educational value.

The "Holocaust Industry" has already inspired polemics. The memorials of this dark page in history are ubiquitous: in Berlin, capital once again, entrusted to the American historian James E. Young, an immense museum similar in nature is under construction. In distant Sydney, a small Jewish Museum of modest proportion and founded five years before the New York one reproduces this triadic structure: on the first floor are some sketches of Australian Jewish history, not far above the anecdotal; the horror on the second floor; and then, the liberation on the third; a truly cathartic experience even at the extreme edges of the world. Beyond the extermination industry's public memorials and edifices that risk appearing cult-like thanks to excessiveness of the "memory" (isn't perhaps history, already on its own, institutionalized memory transformed into writing?), American and European academia produce hundreds of books on the topic. This has come after the overrated success of Daniel Goldhagen's book, which is already covered in gold by its editors for anticipated sales of its next printing. Princeton University has historically never been inclined toward Jewish Studies, with the exception of a few scholars; and yet it is re-launching in pompa magna its Jewish program by asking the renowned Berlin scholar and vehement traditionalist, Peter Schaefer, to direct the program. And Schaefer, inaugurating his mandate, is organizing a gigantic conference dedicated to the sorrowful destiny of the European Jews and the "future of memory." Is it reasonable to ask: What exactly does "future of memory" mean? Is it not rather the "discovery of memory," and the rejection, meditated but also sudden, of a too-long oblivion?

Books that attempt to "understand" and "explain" Hitler are written with haste and fury and published one after another. On the cover of one is a photo of Hitler as a child, handsome just as children usually are (even malicious ones)—an act that explains nothing. Tenure-track positions in Holocaust Studies are created like those for Modern History or Women's Studies. The concern focuses not on whether the subject is inadequate and thereby not worthy of a tenure-track position (perish the thought!), but whether or not it is fashionable, which in the end undermines the true value of the subject, isolating and demonizing it as if it were not demonic enough on its own. It is of little importance that prestigious universities like Harvard or Washington University in St. Louis decline private offers to finance or to create *ex novo* such tenure positions. Serious historians quarrel incessantly amongst themselves over the implications of this horror story. A retired Anglican scholar, Lawrence L. Langer, writes book after book on the Shoah, but more for his own understanding and thus to come to terms with it rather than to explain the reasons of such horror to his readers. He writes obsessively about Primo Levi, his principal icon, explaining that Levi's suicide in 1987 stemmed from his incapacity to understand his survival at Auschwitz forty years earlier. His is an eloquent answer, if in fact true, to the rhetorical question, "What does 'future of memory' mean?"

The future of memory is, precisely, oblivion, not its antithesis. Langer concludes this with apocalyptic tones in his last effort, *Preempting the Holocaust* (Yale University Press, 1998): an unforgivable crime, a single blow, the very incarnation of injustice in this world. Surprisingly, the most decisive attack goes to those who defended, even if weakly, the ethics of forgiveness. This includes Catholic and Protestant theologians, but also, ambiguously, Simon Wiesenthal, the great sleuth, the bloodhound of the surviving Nazis who hid like old wolves and foxes in the farthest, most remote, and at times most inhospitable corners of the world. Langer acts as a moralist on a subject that requires him to take such a stance, a subject that naturally invokes such positions. He writes very well, illuminating episodes and consciousness, but he says nothing new.

Perhaps there is nothing new to be said. More specific questions are considered in books like authors such as Peter Novick, a contemporary historian in Chicago, on the impact of the Holocaust on the lives of Americans and American Jews in the last twenty-five years (*The Holocaust in American Life*, Houghton Mifflin 1999), which Langer reviewed with diffidence in the New York Times Book Review. In the end, the impact of the Holocaust on the American imagination and conscience is less radical than Novick's assertion. He fails to provide convincing evidence. The recognition of the event is linked principally to the Jews, and nevertheless, even amongst themselves, the positions and interpretation vary. It is a book based mostly upon conjecture. For this reason it does not compare to the splendid volume by English historian Tony Kushner, published in 1994 and dedicated to the Holocaust in the liberal imagination and political culture in post-war England.

The problem of this ceaseless flood of research and attention to what may be the blackest period in human history, whose epicenter is located in a country practically untouched by the tragedy — aside from discovering it and observing with utmost disgust and surprise during the first months of 1945 — is divisible into two questions. The first relates to the undeniable scenic and scenographic recollection of the event. The organized extermination of ten million people, six million of whom Jewish, with all the necessary apparatus and paraphernalia, is something extraordinarily attractive, at least to those who, and they are many, have a developed sense of the morbid. This would have been assuredly recognized by the masters of the artistic sublime, from Edmund Burke to Edgar Allan Poe. Consider for example Steven Spielberg, who acts as a patron of this art as well as a director. But there is no certainty that the purely indisputable moral condemnation that accompanies the scenic representations and the museums dedicated to the exterminations serves, in some way, as lessons on morality to the world. Yes, it serves to educate, but undoubtedly also to entertain. The organized trips to the concentration camps and the extermination furnaces, in their squalid state of ruin, have possibly a greater impact than their reproductions in sophisticated hyper-technological frames like those in the American museums. On the other hand, it is difficult to send groups of school children with their backpacks, Cokes and sneakers to walk through Sobibor and Treblinka. There is something speculative, even in the best of intentions, about the creators of these museums. Ignoring it is useless.

The second question, closely tied to the first, deals with the image of Europe we take from this, precisely in the moment in which -- with great effort and with an unsteady economic system -- the European community has established the EU, notably and definitively augmenting its own political identity. And yet, in the United States, where the teaching of European history is increasingly marginalized and reduced in favor of other histories (China, Japan, Africa, Indonesia, Korea) suggestively rediscovered by the tides of "World History" and where as a consequence knowledge of Europe is often limited and trivialized, the value of Europe itself becomes trivialized. The fact that museums are built and dedicated to the history of Europe, but in fact are focused on its most atrocious episode, could be in the long run agonizingly counterproductive.

It is curious that in America they do not build, as they probably should, museums dedicated to the Renaissance or to the Enlightenment, important pages of European history notwithstanding their ambiguities. They do however build museums on the Holocaust, which is not exactly the Old World's finest contribution to humanity. The thought naturally comes to mind that all these museums serve not to bring Europe and the United States closer but to distance Americans from Europeans. And it is stupefying that scholars such as Peter Schaefer, a German, play the game, even if they do so in good faith. The risk is that America will present itself to the universe as "righteous amongst all nations," or to use a Jewish term, the Zadikkim, ascribing to themselves a history of prosperity, versus that of Germany, which had a few raging years of folly and crime (notwithstanding the 250th anniversary of the birth of Goethe) involving Italy, Hungary, the Sudet and numerous other regions, including Central Europe. Museums should be opened on the infinite number of glories in European history—there is an abundance of them from which to choose—including a museum on European Judaism for which one could utilize the manifold documentation to be found in America. To begin with, for example, there is the splendid collection of painted matrimonial contracts dating back to the Italian Renaissance and Baroque periods that are some of the coveted jewels of the Jewish Theological Seminary in New York.

The sublime, as the young Edmund Burke taught us, is not only horror.

6

Following the Hutterites

The unique American destiny of peace and harmony of a Protestant European sect that had a miserable life in the Old World

Suburban America is a place of widespread economic prosperity, increasingly indifferent to horrendous malls mushrooming along its highways and corporate fortresses with an architectonically flat encephalogram; both evolved during the uninterrupted prosperity of past decades. They preserve, notwithstanding the immensity of their spaces, socio-economic and religious niches as peculiar and interesting as they are ancient. Peter Weir's 1985 film *Witness* depicts the serene life of a Protestant community of German origin, the Amish, unnerved by its clash with cynical American society. Kelly McGillis portrays with extreme delicacy a young naive and alluring mother who is attracted to a city man, but because of her religious and rural upbringing rejects him. The man is rough-edged and compassionate but has to be forceful to carry out his role as a policeman in a violent American metropolis.

Thanks to an extraordinary encounter in a house on the state border between New York and Connecticut, on Thanksgiving 1998, between an actor who had an important role in *Witness* and a journalist who thirty years ago inquired into the life of the Hutterites, the idea was born to write this essay. The Hutterites, a group about which journalist Jon Swan wrote a salient piece for *The Atlantic Monthly*, represent a singular aspect of the American dream.

Their history in the Old World was as dark as it is bright in the New World, almost as if to confirm what Tocqueville asserted about the undoubted benefits of religious tolerance—or rather,

The precepts of the 1968 protests are found within the Hutterite community, but these can be found even earlier in the doctrinal texts that are the very basis of their faith. These include Acts 2: 44-45 and 4: 32-35, which can be found on websites about the Hutterites. The verses read: "And all that believed were together, and had all things common; And sold their possessions and goods and parted them as every man had need..." as well as, "...and neither said any of them that ought of the things which he possessed was his own; but that they had all things in common."

Thus were the origins of Christianity right after Christ's death. In 1968, the interest in this type of communal lifestyle spread throughout Europe and America. Essays and academic works about them abounded, such as *Education and Marginality in the Communal Society of the Hutterites* (1965) by J.A. Hostetler; *All Things Common: The Hutterites and Their Way of Life* (1965) by V. Peters; and even translations from German of the communal songs or classics about the Hutterite doctrine, such as "Torches Together by Eberhard Arnold" (1964). But the Hutterites, in accordance with St. Paul's Second Letter to the Colossians (6, 14-18), preached detachment from this world and never responded to the invitations of fraternity from members of the 1968 protest movements.

Jon Swan's 1972 article was a prime example of a circumspect approach that was very respectful toward the archaic community but nevertheless had nothing in common with a part of the confused ideology of 1968: the community of goods did not encourage sexual promiscuity, marriage in fact was highly regarded, and above all, the communal life was sustained by an eminently religious tension. Swan placed an exemplary quote at the beginning of his article: "Without religion sharing doesn't work." The voyage that ended in Bon Homme, the oldest South Dakota colony, provided the reader with an idea of external and internal serenity, but also of separation from the rest of the world. These notions made one wary of any thought of violating the separation or of any attempt to imitate it without having the same spiritual and historical origins. This was a separate world, which should be preserved as such.

Thirty years after Swan's journey, Hutterite life in North America seems to have maintained its aura of separatism and exclusivity even if secularization, a great peril already cautioned against and moderately accepted in 1970, is continuously on the rise. There are evermore frequent and threatening contacts with the "external world", especially among the youth, through various forms of innocent socialization like sports.

In addition to the agricultural products that have always been placed on the local market, some particularly enterprising Hutterites have in recent years expanded into manufacturing. This manufacturing has diversified into machinery, ventilation, carbon heating, and plastics, all for agricultural needs. These small industries are prospering thanks to the laborious nature of the community (typical of European rural communities), of Hutterite mastery, and thanks as well to the cooperative format with which these companies are naturally formed.

The Hutterites have almost doubled in population since 1970. At present they number 36,000 and live in 428 colonies, with an average of about 84 individuals per colony. They have exceeded the demographic development of the average American starting from 1970. Historically, the Hutterites have never been so numerous nor financially secure. They enjoy the prestige of being the oldest religiously-inspired but essentially lay colony in the United States. In the 2020s, they will celebrate 500 years. But, as Swan noted in his article, the Hutterites don't like to party.

Instead, historians will celebrate their 500 years with renewed interest in their unique destiny, following the path of those previously mentioned. They will perhaps rediscover Emil J. Waltner, whose *Banished for Faith* contained some of the writings of an 18th century Hutterite, Johannes Waldner, who wrote the first Hutterite history during the height of the Enlightenment. Published in 1968, *Banished for Faith* signaled a moment of glory—absolutely not sought after nor appreciated—for our Hutterite brothers. The brainchild of one of those many simple, passionate minds in Europe during the Reformation, in the small village of Moos, in South Tyrol, finds its descendents spread throughout South Dakota, Minnesota, Montana, Washington, and Alberta, still faithful to his original message and thought.

II

On Men, Poets, and Presidents (and not only)

With all its growing collectivism, America still remains the ideal place for individuals. This section of the book is divided into five chapters. Every year, or maybe every second year of American history since 1787, there are books, discussions, exhibitions, and polemics regarding the Founding Fathers. It happened also in 1998-1999, and two of the following essays are devoted to George Washington (normally absolutely praised and never contested) and to Thomas Jefferson (normally, as an intellectual first, more contested than praised). They are based on a celebratory exhibition on Washington at the Huntington and on a book of polemics about Jefferson.

    The other three chapters deal with unusual figures. One, Uncle Sam, is completely imaginary and is based on an exhibition about this truly American icon held at the New York Historical Society. One chapter is devoted to Vassar Miller. If ordinary people solidly make America, some of them turn into extraordinary writers. Miller, who died in 1999, was a gifted poet who was affected by a severe physical disability. Her lore reminded me of an Italian poet, Alda

Merini, who died while I was writing these pages in November 2009. The first essay, drawn from a couple of obituaries in the *New York Times*, has been inspired by Plutarch. While the great Greek writer wrote a number of "parallel lives," I devoted an essay to a couple of deaths, verily parallel, which occurred in 1998-1999. These were the deaths of the architect Charles Luckman, who died on January 24th, 1999, and Wassily Leontief, an economist, who died on February 5th, 1999. Although as a libertarian thinker I place myself rather far from Leontief's views, and I still identify the prototype of the architect and pioneer of freethinking as Ayn Rand's masterpiece character Howard Roark, both Luckman and Leontief can be regarded as true American heroes. This is even more so, because like Rand, Leontief was born in Saint Petersburg in 1905. They both lived long, successful lives, one winning a Nobel Prize, and contributed strongly to America's take-off after 1945.

7

Parallel Deaths

The concurrent end of an architect and of an economist, protagonists of the American Dream

There are icons, images, concepts, and even prejudices that characterize the American mentality of the past century—the "American Century"—with roots embedded in the Colonial experiences of the New World. These are ideas such as "pragmatism" and "activism," which seem to dominate the American mentality and are manifest in the emphasis placed on extreme attention to detail. They are also the ability to communicate succinctly and therefore effectively, to use the past in a utilitarian way, and to use the future in an oracular way—a "vision" of the future that enables, presumably, its manipulation and subsequent domination. Within weeks of each other, two luminaries, in their respective ways emblematic of this mentality, died. Both passed softly in their old age, one on the Pacific Coast and the other on the Atlantic, in two symbolic American cities, different, but at the same time similar: Los Angeles and New York.

Charles Luckman died in Los Angeles on January 24th, 1999. He was eighty-nine years old and, for many years, had been the prime target of American conservationism. Responsible for the demolition of the old, elegant, and glorious Penn Station, the largest train station in New York, he subsequently constructed the imposing black cylinder Madison Square Garden. Luckman once stated, "I am firm in my opinion that architecture is a business and not an art." This was admirable candor for a man who grew up during the Great Depression and whose marketing and advertising skills were so unique that in 1937, he was featured on the cover of *Time* as the prodigy child of American industry. He was just twenty-seven years old.

With success after success, Luckman's career captured the dilemma of commercial architecture in the past century, a century in which functionalism, pragmatism, essentiality, and the necessity to save—all admirable qualities—sufficed. Consequently, this was a century in which bad taste, shameful aesthetics, and stylistic indecency ran the risk of offending those who worked in such a building; and, to a lesser degree, also those who found themselves looking upon it everyday. Where and when does one draw the line between the former and the latter?

In reality, Luckman, who focused on the absence of ornament (who knows if he ever considered Adolf Loos's golden book), proved that in art even the most extreme approach to functionalism could be a form of artistic expression. Luckman's idea of "art" was too narrow, and it was this narrow idea that he opposed, not "art" in the larger sense. He was, if not the designer, the patron of the Lever House in New York, the first imposing glass skyscraper in the Big Apple. Later he designed with his studio the Prudential Center in Boston, a squared elevated glass tower situated almost directly on the Boston shoreline. Resolute in its sobriety and efficiency, it still blends easily into the unassuming skyline of the most culturally refined city in the United States.

Faced with certain extravagances or with the *involuntary* lack of imagination in corporate American architecture, one almost misses Luckman's "programmed" absence of imagination and decoration. He would perhaps not even appreciate that his works were considered "beautiful." But many of his works, like the Prudential Center, are in fact beautiful. Those who seek beauty do not always obtain it; but often, those who, for *parti pris*, shun such a goal produce surprisingly beautiful pieces. In the last years of his life, Luckman donated several millions of dollars to create a center of fine and applied arts in his name. Upon the inauguration of the center at California State University, he commented that the intention of his donation was to recognize that there was too much emphasis on business and the "down to earth" approach in art. For Luckman, it was time to take a deep breath and remember that we established this country thanks also to culture. This extraordinary conversion recalls that of the libertines like Casanova, who declared themselves Christians on their deathbeds.

Parallel Deaths 39

In New York on February 5, 1999, at the ripe age of 93, Wassily Leontief passed away. In 1973 he had won the Nobel Prize for Economics. He taught until a late age—for better or for worse, at private American universities there is no compulsory retirement age. In this case, it was for fortune's sake that Leontief actively taught at New York University until his death.

A child of the imperial Old World, Leontief was born in Saint Petersburg in the fateful year of 1905, the year that gave the first signs of revolution inexorably leading to Red October in 1917. A professor at Harvard for 44 continuous years, Leontief won the Nobel Prize for his input-output theory. This theory played a role not only in economics, but also entered the realm of political and everyday jargon. With sophisticated analysis, Leontief brought to light a method for indicating how the effects of varied productivity within a specific sector could impact the entire cycle of global economic production. To oversimplify, given a certain input, such as a production crisis in a small sector, there would be a certain output or a series of outputs, which are more or less calculable, on a wide scale across the world economy. Large companies like General Electric have successfully used this descriptive forecasting model.

Leontief's economic theories and his personality were strongly oriented toward practice and reality, and he was always prepared to fold in the face of empirical data rather than forcing it and himself to fit a preconceived theory. Of the importance of concrete data, he stated,

"Facts. You have to have facts. Theories aren't good unless you have facts to back them." He also recommended to economists, almost as Marx did to philosophers (as did Nietzsche—who invited them to board ships), to immerse themselves in the real world, in the reality of industries and companies rather than spend the day brooding over books and vague theories. His was a somewhat excessive position, and perhaps a combination of both theory and experience would be the best solution for an economist. Nonetheless, Leontief coherently maintained this position throughout his whole career.

After his studies in Berlin, with Nazism on the rise, Leontief immigrated to the States and almost immediately commenced his brilliant career at Harvard. Certainly, his theories were not *laissez-*

faire. He hoped, more or less covertly, for the state to have operative (and not only informative) controls on the economy, for he believed that his theory was applicable everywhere. Perhaps this approach was a remnant from his years of study in Berlin, where for centuries political economics viewed the state as its center, as the end of all action and all speculation. In reality, Leontief was a long way from "statism" of any political nature. He simply thought that his model of economic preventive control could be practiced, above all, by an entity economically independent and in a certain sense, *super partes*, exactly like the state. What is not clear is whether the state should act as a simple consultant, providing economic strategies derived from the systematic application of the input-output theory, or if instead the state should impose such strategies. Leontief never revealed a penchant for socialism: he simply intended his model to serve as a preventive analytical measure to avoid periods of recession. History has demonstrated that similar hopes are utopist and, above all, always appear clearer than the real economic situation. In fact, in an age of globalization, the economy follows its own difficult-to-foresee course. Leontief's economic planning did not consist of totalitarianism, but rather pure naïveté.

Luckman and Leontief died leaving America profoundly different than when they found it, in part thanks to their contribution: two men so distant yet so close. They would both probably be uncomfortable in America today, an America that is starting to fear the end of a decade of uninterrupted prosperity. Even if it is not clear how this ending will come, there are already signs, both visible and invisible, in these interminable horizons. Maybe personages such as these two belong to the past. Maybe America, by now satiate, no longer feels the need for a pragmatic reality but rather desires a contemplative one. I imagine that Luckman and Leontief will warn me from heaven of the devastating effects of contemplation, and yet, contemplation appears to many Americans (and not only) like a mirage in the desert.

8

That "Great Experiment" Called the U.S.A.

An exhibition at the Huntington Library celebrates the second centennial of the death of George Washington

On December 14th, 1799, George Washington died at Mount Vernon, his grand estate, at the age of sixty-seven. Two hundred years later, America commemorated his death with various exhibitions and lectures, which took place everywhere in this great country that he, more than anyone else, helped to create. One of these exhibitions, perhaps not the most lavish but certainly with merit, was inaugurated in 1998 in one of the most magnificent places in the United States—the Huntington Library of San Marino, California. It is interesting that one of the last states to enter the Union now celebrated that son of Virginia, the oldest state, where English colonists first set foot at the beginning of the 17th century. These men and women paved the way for the colonization of North America and created, through the pages of John Smith, myths that return every so often, like the tale of Pocahontas. Above all, they created the "myth" of the American dream: virgin land of infinite riches, at least in her promises.

Today, if before entering the exhibition one takes a stroll through the Huntington Gardens, one understands that the "American Dream," as George Washington envisioned it—liberty, democracy and well being, if not for all at least for some—has come true. This was true for Henry Huntington, for example, who at the beginning of the last century created an earthly paradise, a park that extends for a seemingly unlimited space. It contains an infinite variety of plants and garden styles, ranging from Japanese and Zen, to Italian and English; it is a marvelous and almost enrapturing collection of exotic and lush plants, from the most rarefied Australian trees to the colossal flora of the North American forests. Next to the gardens, visited annually by millions of tourists, is a center for studies in American Colonialism, the European Renaissance, and English painting in the Georgian era. In short, Huntington Gardens and the Huntington Library are a generous display of patronage to the fine arts. It would be difficult to find a counterpart in America and nearly impossible in Europe. For Huntington, for many generations of Americans, and for the "millions, which are not yet born" (in the celebrated words of the first President of the United States), George Washington's plan for America was accomplished.

If you walk through the rooms and the hallways of the exhibition, you will not find anything new, but you will find a well-organized exhibition of artifacts and letters that document an extraordinary career. The letters date back to his early twenties, when Washington was already in command of the English Army in Virginia and successfully combating the French. In these letters, Washington corresponded with his future allies in the Ohio Campaign. There are also private pieces, such as the jewels he regularly gave to his wife (Washington always lived like an English gentleman from the countryside, abundant in wealth but never in ostentation or vulgarity), which reflect the sober tastes of the great general. John Rhodehamel, curator of rare documents and manuscripts of the American Colonial period at the Huntington Library, edited the exhibition catalogue with acumen. In the brief introduction, Gordon S. Wood, one of the most renowned historians of the American War for Independence, introduces us to the First American President.

It was Washington's destiny to become a hero well before he died. At a young age he was already an icon for his unattainable status as both an individual and a politician. He had the charisma of a true leader, including a certain obtuseness and lack of culture and wit, as his more cultivated (and slightly jealous) comrade and close friend Thomas Jefferson maliciously suggested in his writings. Washington was tall and handsome, he knew how to dance and ride a horse perfectly, and he was a great general (even if he never won an important battle, contrary to Caesar and Napoleon, to whom he often was compared). He did not need to become rich through politics, for he was independently wealthy. He also cultivated an

18th century idea of "virtue" in all its aspects, from military virtue to the virtue of good manners, which he learned at a young age by reading the Italian classics of etiquette. According to Wood, he was the "only true American hero"; not a seducer like Jefferson, nor irascible and passionate like Hamilton or cautious and speculative like George Mason. His winning move was to distance himself from politics—a new Cincinnatus—at the culmination of his power in 1783, the year the military phase of the American War for Independence ended and the year of Yorktown and the definitive defeat of the Redcoats. The motherland finally gave into the new nation's values. Her only remaining act was to negotiate the gains and the losses of England's colonies. Washington was everything but an egotistical calculator; nonetheless, this grand *coup de théâtre* favored him enormously when he was elected the first President of the United States.

Like Jefferson, Madison, and all of the "Founding Fathers," this champion of liberty lived quite lavishly thanks to the labor of some three hundred slaves. This, however, was not a problem back then, or at least, it was not considered as such. Liberty and equality were for free-born white males. Washington was a man of the old regime. He died in 1799, almost prophetically. Although many, above all the Federalists, desired that he run for the 1800 presidential race, Washington did not plan to do so. Much of the "new" course of American politics was completely foreign to him, as he observed the slow passage from a system in which politics were run by leaders and their charisma to a system in which the key players were parties. Washington, who held the English political tradition in high esteem even if England had been his nemesis, should have realized that this type of transition was typical of constitutional regimes and even more so of a pure democracy like America, the one that he himself helped to create.

Naturally, upon his death, America mourned. The greatest, most honorable and universally cherished leader had departed. He was loved by the masses for the very same glacial demeanor that distanced him from the masses. Congressman Henry Lee said that Washington was the "first in war, first in peace and first in the hearts of his countrymen."

A more truthful observation could not have been made. No other president has ever achieved the status of living legend. America now more than ever needs the return of charismatic figures to the White House: to my understanding, neither Gore nor Bradley nor Bush Jr., and especially not the former First Lady (Hillary Rodham Clinton), can challenge Washington's charisma. America has always loved its presidents, and it needs one that evokes its first—though perhaps not one crossing the savage currents of the Delaware with a frozen and wind-burnt face and an air of war and glory. However, neither do Americans need a president scurrying through the halls of the White House with his pants at his knees, hoping not to have been seen petting a passing intern.

In the well-stated words of Gordon Wood, "Washington was an extraordinary man who made it possible for ordinary man to rule." With great discretion and style, this exhibition brings to mind that in moments of crisis, extraordinary men are needed to govern nations and make it possible for future generations of ordinary men to have the opportunity to take the reins of power. prodigy child of American industry. He was just twenty-seven.

9

The True Story of Uncle Sam

A small exhibition at the New York Historical Society illustrates the birth and history of one of the most popular American icons

One arrives at the imposing, soberly neoclassical building of the New York Historical Society by passing the lower side of Central Park. After enduring the sultriness of Fifth Avenue and the tropical humidity of Central Park, the pleasantly cool and dry Calvinist interior of the Society is as welcome as manna. There is something contradictory about an exhibition on Uncle Sam here. The New York Historical Society is on 77th West, across from the Museum of Natural History, but also next to some of the most luxurious condos in New York City. These are pre-war buildings, colossal and rather unimaginative, but which house apartments worth millions, discretely watched over by gruff doormen who pass their time parking the luxurious cars of the wealthy and chatting with one another, usually in Spanish.

This is a decided contrast with the austere figure of Uncle Sam. Since the mid-19th century when he became a national icon, Uncle Sam has embodied the idea of parsimony, sobriety, rigor, and discipline with his sharp features, tall stature, and white beard — the appropriate guise for a fanatic preacher from William Penn's flotilla. These are two of the innumerable spirits of America: the luxury of 77th Street and the old-fashioned, and perhaps bygone, sobriety of Uncle Sam.

But when was Uncle Sam born? Legend has it that a man named Samuel Wilson was born in Arlington, Massachusetts. It seems that during the 1812 war, Sam worked in Troy, New York, as a meat supplier to the troops. On the crates of meat arriving at the front lines was written "U.S.," a new denomination for the United States. It was later claimed that many soldiers thought that "U.S." referred to Uncle Sam, and thus the legend was born. In 1959 the legend was solidified when the city of Troy petitioned to Congress to be recognized as the official city of Uncle Sam, regardless of the fact that Wilson was born in Arlington. The petition was granted, and for the small city in upstate New York, named after the classical city symbolic of defeat and the disappearance of an entire civilization, it was a great recompense to be recognized as the official homeland of an American icon. Now it could consider itself equal to the other cities of upstate New York, honored with such names as Athens, Rome, and Ithaca.

Uncle Sam has slowly pushed aside the other symbols of America: Lady Liberty, Brother Jonathan, and Yankee Doodle. With Brother Jonathan there had been a certain overlap of roles until the mid-19th century, when Uncle Sam became a symbol of government and Brother Jonathan the archetype of the common American. This image was later forgotten, and Uncle Sam took its place. Uncle Sam was made famous to the world by the war poster by James Montgomery Flagg, with the phrase, "I want YOU for the U.S. Army." This is an ungrammatical phrase, as Sarah Bayliss has noted in the *New York Times*. His dry, severe, intimidating face has remained a part of the American imagination since that 1917 poster. Uncle Sam is above all a symbol of fidelity to the homeland and of the necessity to sacrifice for one's country. The state propaganda machine made ample use of his image not only during the First World War, but also during the Second, with increasingly refined posters, figures, and messages that were direct but with a good dose of subtlety for the day.

Top advertising agencies in voluntary service to the nation have given various memorable versions of Uncle Sam, beginning with Young & Rubicam in 1912. Apart from Flagg, the author of the most celebrated image, numerous other illustrators have depicted this lanky David Crockett, so good-naturedly threatening (or perhaps threateningly good-natured). Others range from Nelson B. Greene to Cecil Calvert Beall to Joseph Keppler and from Thomas Nast to Homer Davenport. A 1918 poster by Schneck, designed after the sinking of the *Lusitania*, depicted the only vaguely disturbing female presence that ever got near the Puritan Sam. This presence was created to feminize America, who, dejected and in disarray at the feet of an irate Sam, implored, "It's up to you to protect the nation's honor." The United States had just entered into war.

But even before 1917, Uncle Sam played a fundamental role in political propaganda, often with a conservative voice. During the Civil War, Sam was clearly a Unionist; he was physically similar to Abraham Lincoln. A splendid series of envelopes for Union troops used as letterhead magnificent vignettes in which Sam showed his ability to win the war. Following the Spanish-American War in 1898, Sam became the protagonist of comic strips in the conservative satirical magazine *Puck*. In particular, Sam and a hypothetical Lady America showed both their reluctance toward immigration (of Cubans, Filipinos, Hawaiians, and Puerto Ricans) and their opposition to an American foreign policy too inclined to aid poorer nations. Two posters from *Puck* in 1898 succinctly illustrate such positions: "Goodwill begins at home" by Louis Dalrymple and "A Shadow of Embarrassment" by Joseph Keppler, Jr. Uncle Sam, therefore, played a role beyond official government politics. Even presidential candidates and minor politicians abundantly exploited the icon "without copyright," including Roosevelt.

Radical pacifists also enlisted Uncle Sam during Vietnam. A celebrated photograph shows a very particular Uncle Sam, chubby and in good spirit, at a peace demonstration in Central Park in 1968. Here the poet Allen Ginsberg, physically the antithesis of classic Uncle Sam with his glasses and long, black, curly hair, read antiwar poetry and waved the Stars and Stripes. Uncle Sam also entered into the avant-garde with Andy Warhol's memorable representation, estranged and full of paradox, in a series of works dedicated to American icons, in which Warhol included, besides himself, Mickey Mouse and the Wicked Witch of the West.

Sam, therefore, moves and transforms with America, even if today the numerous publicity campaigns to increase military enrollment find him nearly obsolete and instead use more direct and youthful images taken from action films. Nevertheless, his appeal continues to be utilized, for example, in ads for the tax software Turbotax. From the beginning of the 20th century, that lanky man with the white beard, gruff to the point of excess but fundamentally of great humanity and optimal sentiment, has served to advertise goods of the most varying range, including an Ex-Lax laxative in the 1920s. His image was occasionally used in the 19th century, once even to advertise oysters. This brings to mind the 1925 quote by Calvin Coolidge that the curators of the New York Historical Society exhibition have included in the wall text: "The chief business of American people is business." The prototype of the American, Uncle Sam, in the end could not contradict such spirit. Who knows if some descendant of Sam Wilson doesn't live in one of the million dollar lofts situated next to the New York Historical Society, in spite of every possible contradiction?

10

Disability and Poetry: A Homage to Vassar Miller

The death of a poet who was afflicted with cerebral palsy, author of splendid and yet not well-known verses

In memory of Rosanna Benzi (Genova, Italy, 1949-1991)

Discreetly, at the Methodist Hospital in Houston on the last day of October 1998, Vassar Miller died. She was seventy-four years old, although her constricted and suffered expression made her seem older. She departed from the state and the city that she had rarely ever left: the rich, vital, and only seemingly arid Texas, a state that named her poet laureate twice and that boasted of her as one of its greatest literary achievements. Outside of Texas her poetry was not well-known, and outside of the United States she was not known at all. Nationally, with the exception of the finalist nomination for the Pulitzer Prize in 1961, her name was rarely mentioned or recognized. Miller did not belong to a particular school of thought or of poetry, and she had developed a poetic style that was all her own: profoundly intimate and openly religious, so much so that often her poems were mistaken for prayers, and rightly so. Her sickness spurred deep within her a love for the small joys in life: writing and reading verse, lining herself up next to the ice cream vendors in her wheelchair on a hot day in torrid Houston or sipping chocolate sorbet in the shade.

For a woman that described her meaning in life as the duty "to write and to serve God," with a significant precedence given to "writing," certainly her poetry will be remembered, and her fame, achieved only at the end of her life, will endure. In a country where the disabled minorities receive more social attention than in

Europe, where ramps to libraries and to public restrooms are still rarities even in the most advanced complexes, Miller distinguished herself for her efforts in favor of the disabled in a personal way. Her activity was much in the manner of the Genoese Rosanna Benzi, an outspoken advocate of the disabled until about ten years ago when death freed Benzi from her iron lung.

In 1985 Miller edited a volume of verses and stories dedicated to and written by the disabled. In striking comparison with the stories, which were illuminating but at times disturbing and cruel, the volume was preceded by an equally illuminating but serene preface, with acute observations:

> The handicapped have, to a large extent, come out of the back bedroom, to which an ignorant past has relegated them. The purpose of this anthology is to ensure also that the disabled come out of the back bedroom of the mind and so liberate not only the captives but also the captors. For any jail, however benign, imprisons jailor as well as jailed.

The anthology, entitled *Despite This Flesh*, includes a drawing of a figure standing with his arms crossed in meditation, seemingly estranged and hurt. The artist is David A. Sampson, also afflicted with cerebral palsy. There are small gems of poetry like "Seated Nude" by Richard Ronan, which describes the carnal intensity between a man in a wheelchair and a "normal" woman, echoing the descriptions in the anti-Vietnam film *Coming Back Home*. But it is Miller's poetic activity that will remain in the American consciousness and hopefully also in its literature. The complete collection of her poetry, *If I had Wheels or Love*, was published in 1990 and includes all of her previously released works, from *Adams's Footprints* (1956) to *Struggling to Swim on Concrete* (1984). There is also the splendid collection published in that fateful '68 titled *Onions and Roses*. The collection's brief introduction by the critic George Garrett describes well the itinerarium of Miller's poetry, including her experimentation for more open poetic forms, her progressive emancipation from her own style (her earlier poems being somewhat too rigid and homiletic), and her increasingly discrete attention, occasionally even reception, toward what the American literary panorama was formulating and discussing. Naturally, pain and death were central themes in Miller's poetry.

The description of a dying woman in her first collection (1956) echoes Kavafis; perhaps he entered Miller's poetic repertoire in her youth. The final verses, which regard the alienation of the dying conceivably more than that of the corpse itself, could well be placed in a new edition of Norbert Elias's essay on the solitude of the dying in our times. Elias's essay has constituted a classic for sociology and cultural criticism (and which is full of T. W. Adorno's echoes).

> Her spirit hiding among skin and bones
> In willingness and wariness waits death
> Like hares that peer from corners of their pens
> Lured by a curiosity, yet loath.
> Her eyes meet bed, chair, face, but do not focus.
> As if these objects, heretofore mere shade,
> Have caught up with their shadows. Things that wake us
> Upon her eyelids heap a heavy load.
> As straws pierce rock, our words reach where she lies,
> Heedless of our cheerfulness or condolence.
> Uncaring how out chatter ebbs or flows,
> She catches the first syllable of silence.
> So true the craftsman, memory, in lying
> She will be less a stranger dead than dying.

Because of a nearly imperceptible irony, Miller's poetry does not aspire to be prayer, despite its religiosity. She prefers the solid ground of a contemplative, and at times vivacious, poetry. In her second collection, *Wage War on Silence* (1960), one finds this singular "*Cantico delle Creature*" ode, *Love Song for the Future*:

> To our ruined vineyards come,
> Little foxes, for your share
> Of our blighted grapes, the tomb
> Readied for our common lair.
> Ants, we open you the cupboard;
> Flee no more the heavy hand
> Harmless as a vacant scabbard

Since your homes like ours are sand.
Catamounts so often haunted,
Wend your ways through town or city,
Since both you and we are haunted
By the Weird Ones with no pity.
Deer and bear we used to stalk,
We would spend our dying pains
Nestling you with mouse and hawk
Near our warmth until it wanes.

Weave across our faces, spiders,
Webwork fragile as flower;
Welcome, serpents, subtle gliders,
For your poison fails in power.
Loathed no longer, learn your worth,
Toad and lizard, snail and eel –
Remnant of a living earth
Cancelled by a world of steel,

Whose miasmic glitter dances
Over beast's and man's sick daze
While our eyes which scored St. Francis
Watch Isaiah's vision craze:
Ox and lion mingling breath
Eat the straw of doom; in tether
To the selfsame stake of death
Wolf and lamb lie down together.

During a trip to Italy, Miller wrote one of her most touching lyrical compositions, "The Protestant Cemetery in Florence", placed at the inception of her collection *Onions and Roses*. The poem, beginning with the reading of an eccentric epitaph placed on a tomb in the Protestant cemetery and often visited by poets, lovers, and guests, empathetically and majestically reconstructs the fatal destiny of Victorian Englishwoman who fell victim to melancholic love and the effluvia of morphine.

Exiled with you a moment on this island
Whose lushness folds the stark bones of the dead,
I envy you your breathless flight to Florence,
Till I recall that nothing's quite so simple,
That tables turned will wrench the stoutest heart.
For I remember how you in a letter
Wrote, "Father could have kept me had he loved me
More openly," – dark secrets future doctors
Would probe for offered on your outspread palm.
And you took morphine till the day you died,
Though less than formerly, Italian sunshine
More curative in poems than in life.
You sought out conversation with the spirits,
An anodyne to heady draughts of flesh
Under whose influence you conceived a child
A fact to scare a small Victorian girl
Of forty-some-odd years more than ghosts could.
"And I, who looked for only God, found you,"
You sonneteered to Robert, paying God
Rather a backhand compliment that even
A jealous Jehovah would not mind much,
Since Robert himself proved scarcely sufficient.
You looked behind you always, back toward death
Wherein along you could have borne to hear
Your brother's names, love never having borne
The heavy past away. So I pronounce
Your epitaph carved from the facts which arch
Your grave, "Nothing is final. Only this."

For poetry, as Robert Schumann maintained regarding music, there is no better introduction and explanation than the piece itself. An epitaph worthy of Miller is a 1980s poem from her later collection from which the collection takes its title, *If I Had Wheels or Love*. At the time Vassar was losing the use of her upper body, which made her progressively, painfully, unable to write—that natural gesture that she skillfully describes. Written for her friend Joanne Avinger, but "not only" as is specified in the dedication, the poem follows a classical scheme composed of five tercets and a closing quatrain. Employing classical imagery, she describes the pain that is similar to when the serpent carrying the name of Sickness grasped Laocoön in his coils. While physically crushing him to death, the serpent does not obstruct him from saving flights of mind and emotion:

If I Had Wheels or Love

I could make prayers or poems on and on,
Relax or labor all the summer day,
If I had wheels or love, I would be gone.

Spinning along the roadsides into dawn,
Feeling the flesh of lovers whom I'd lay
I could make prayers or poems on and on.

Whistling the hours by me as they drone,
Kissed on my breast and belly where I'd play
If I had wheels or love, I would be gone.

Over the next horizon toward the sun,
Deep in the shadows where I found the way
I could make prayers or poems on and on.

Along the country backgrounds flower-strewn,
Fondling your flanks, my dear, made clouds from clay.
If I had wheels or love, I would be gone.

Cool as the evening is and soft as fawn,
Warm as my fiddling fingers when they say
I could make prayers or poems on and on.
If I had wheels or love, I would be gone.

11

An American Sphinx

Thomas Jefferson's inexhaustible attractiveness in the American imagination

In October 1992 America celebrated, or rather, attempted to avoid celebrating America's discovery by shifting the focus from Christopher Columbus to Europe in 1492. The celebrated exhibition *Circa 1492*, held in Washington D.C. and in New York, discussed European art, politics, science, and culture from the late 15th century. For the sake of political correctness, almost as prevailing then as it is today, the exhibition ignored Columbus's discovery of America. This discovery opened the path to several invasions that brought great suffering and almost annihilated the indigenous population that had contact with the *conquistadores*, with their germs, their weapons, their *perros corazados*, and their violence. While the intelligentsia and academia concentrated on what many consider the unfortunate landing at Hispaniola (modern day Haiti) on October 12th five centuries ago, another distinctively different historiography, belonging to the "ordinary people," was in preparation. This was the celebration of the birth of Thomas Jefferson, a man who became a sort of American icon during his lifetime, second only to, according to inexplicable and oscillating classifications, his contemporary George Washington and perhaps Abraham Lincoln.

Thomas Jefferson was born in April 1743, but already by the end of 1992 Americans began to celebrate his birth for the following year. The University of Virginia hosted the celebratory conference, with the apparently neutral title: "Jeffersonian Legacies." The school, which Jefferson founded and designed, is a neoclassical and almost tropical paradise, strewn with statues of the third president on the fragrant grounds, situated in Charlottesville, VA.

The conference was not simply celebratory. Instead, it was held in the usual American manner of trying its icons' moral weaknesses before the court of conscience and ethics. In fact, there were two singular events. The first was the explicit attack upon the moral stature of Jefferson. Paul Finkelman, a historian from Virginia Tech, discussed Jefferson's most apparent contradiction, for which the red-haired and lanky Thomas himself was in perennial conflict. As Finkelman put it, how could a man such as Jefferson, who drafted the Declaration of Independence, a revolutionary, liberal document with respect to human rights (he was thirty-three years old, the perfect age to do miraculous things), which proclaimed that all men were created equal, possess slaves and behave for the rest of his political and personal life with extraordinary ambiguity regarding blacks and abolition? This was, after all, the document that inspired the French *Declaration of Rights of Man and of the Citizen* of 1789, except that the French replaced God the Creator with nature: "all men are born equal."

Without doubt, this is a legitimate question, and one that denotes a far greater propensity of Americans (whether or not historians) to criticize their "Founding Fathers." Americans especially compare the founders to the Machiavellian, permissive, or indifferent Europeans, in both Jefferson's time and even today. It is quite legitimate to ask oneself why this landowner, intellectual, and distinguished politician could have allowed himself to fall into such an evident contradiction. He never became an abolitionist, at least not publicly; however, in private, in his only completed work, *Notes on the State of Virginia*, he decries the horrific institution of slavery, at times with passionate lucidity. Nonetheless, it took half a century and Abraham Lincoln, a president completely different from Jefferson and neither as intellectual nor as cosmopolitan, to achieve Jefferson's aristocratic liberalism: the emancipation of the slaves, which led America to its only, but bloody, Civil War.

Certainly, Jefferson's lucid mind must have perceived that the institution of slavery was degrading, inhumane, and contrary to human rights. In fact, as a scholar of the French Enlightenment and friend of several Enlightenment thinkers, he boasted of understanding and applying their doctrine. He must also have understood, however, that for a long time to come, slavery would permit the growth of the new nation, which had the potential for extreme prosperity, but which at the time and for the foreseeable future was inundated by debt and unable to exploit its own resources. Therefore, even though humanly and legally (from the point of view of natural rights, or, in the end, from a moral point of view) inexcusable, slavery needed to remain for a certain period of time, though ideally without the universally recounted cruelty. So, next to Thomas's splendid neoclassical mansion placidly located on that hill, not without some comfort from the shade of the manor must have been Uncle Tom's cabin.

After Professor Finkelman finished his paper, Robert Cooley, a middle-aged man with a strong Southern accent, who, despite a certain attention to his language and style, probably belonged to the black lower-middle class, entered the conference room. Perhaps he had been invited, perhaps he had been inspired by the eloquent conference title, but he stated with simplicity, "I am a direct descendent of Thomas Jefferson." Silence engulfed the room, yet no one was surprised.

The romantic element unfailingly comes to the fore. Is it true that Jefferson had as his lover one of his slaves, a mulatto woman named Sally Hemmings, about whom we know very little? Since Jefferson's day, this has been the great conundrum to historians, but even more so to the public. His political adversaries accused him of this *liaison dangereuse*. At first he vehemently rebutted the charge, and every time thereafter he closed himself off in a disdainful silence. If one really thinks about it from a historical perspective, demonstrating the existence of this love story is of little import. But obviously the American public has always been keen on presidential sex scandals (between Jefferson and Clinton there have been plenty of interesting "affairs" excluding, of course, the only Abraham Lincoln; no one would ever imagine that algid though enlightened soul lightheartedly chasing skirts). As such, the public has never ceased posing this intriguing question. Naturally, historians have raised this question as well, but apart from a few exceptions, Jefferson scholars resolutely negated the possibility. These exceptions have usually come from somewhat eccentric authors, such as Fawn M. Brodie, who in 1974 justified the relationship between Tom and Sally based upon Freudian motives. However, one must consider

Dumas Malone, who with inexhaustible passion dedicated his entire life to studying Jefferson, producing a multi-volume biography that is the standard text for secondary sources on him today.

In one of the volumes, Malone, who died in 1986, resolutely asserts that an affair with Sally in any manner was unthinkable given the moral criteria by which Jefferson conducted his daily life, and, more importantly, his obsessive commemoration of his dead wife. She died at a young age when Thomas himself was only thirty-nine years old, throwing him into an abyssal depression in which he promised to never re-marry—a promise to which he held true. For this reason, one finds the words Malone uses to describe the relationship, calling it "a vulgar relationship that his family would have eventually discovered" very irritating. If in fact there had been a relationship, why would it have been a "vulgar" one?

This naturally irritated black public opinion, which had never been fond of Jefferson, but at least had celebrated his virility believing that the story with Sally was true. Can a healthy thirty-nine year old man really renounce sexual and sentimental relationships for the rest of his life? Historians, in the absence of documentation, tend to support Malone's position; it is not clear whether the support stems from reverence for the master or for Jefferson or perhaps to both, but if it were out of respect for Jefferson's memory then some moral discredit belongs, more than to Jefferson, to these historians.

Consider the last salient work on Jefferson, Joseph Ellis' *The American Sphinx: The Character of Thomas Jefferson*, a brilliant reconstruction of Jefferson's psychological profile and an extremely pleasurable read, before discussing his political and intellectual character. In the final analysis Ellis is quite skeptical that such a relationship took place. Thus, in a book dedicated to Jefferson's character, which in reality would seem to have been quite moody and very vain, the conclusion is that he would not have been inclined to such a relationship thanks to those very qualities. In the book's appendix in *A Note on the Sally Hemmings Scandal*, Ellis textually confirms:

> What Hamilton and both Adamses understood about Jefferson, and what my own immersion in the historical evidence

has caused me to conclude as well, is that for the most of his adult life he lacked the capacity for the direct and physical expression of his sexual energies. Henry Adams put it more explicitly when he said that Jefferson's temperament was 'almost feminine.'

Aside from the fact that the Adamses did not hold Jefferson in high regard, and the dislike was transmitted through blood and political lines, to connect the lack of sexual appetite to a 'feminine' temperament would make feminists shudder, and not only them. Do only heterosexual males express their sexuality directly?

In any case, Ellis wrote a stimulating and vivid book where a real flesh-and-blood person emerges, as well as many healthy considerations on the use of scandal in politics and historiography. Ellis's book was published in 1997 shortly before another, perhaps final, chapter in the Hemmings saga occurred. Not far away from Mount Holyoke College where Ellis teaches, Eugene A. Foster, a retired professor and a famous pathologist from Tufts University with a passionate interest in American history, decided to carry out a scientific experiment. Generally, when other sciences arrive at conclusions regarding our past, they are disturbing enough to silence most historiographies and almost all of its ideological uses. For instance, thanks to geneticists like Luca Cavalli Sforza, today we know of humankind's single genetic origin, or rather single cell cluster, which is a discovery that should be strong enough to silence all racism.

At the end of 1998, Foster, the retired pathologist, compared the DNA of Jefferson's descendents with that of the African Americans who also claimed to be his descendents. The results: positive. Jefferson, at the youthful age of sixty-five, fathered Eston Hemmings. The results were published in a brief article (in the traditional scientific manner, salient discoveries occupy few pages and, at times, just a few lines, or simply the space necessary to express a formula), which appeared in the prestigious science periodical Nature. Well, if at sixty-five years of age he was able to impregnate Hemmings, it certainly was not due to a "bout" of youthfulness (such as using a bit of Spanish Fly, traditional Viagra of the time, but with much more unpleasant side effects) but, more than likely, was the product of a sexual relationship that seems to have lasted thirty-eight years. The Tom and Sally love story, to which a romantic internet site is dedicated, is true.

Speculations, deductions, reconstructions, intuitions, and elaborations are all invalidated when faced with genetically coded evidence. The question, however, is something else. Apart from sexual intercourse, did they love each other? In this regard a study of Jefferson's character could be useful and, certainly, a relationship which lasted as long as theirs could not have only been based on something as banal as pure sexual instinct. This DNA can never prove.

Just as the dried sperm on Monica Lewinsky's clothes can only tell us that a sexual act occurred, it is still more than likely that the yellowish liquid belonged to Bill. Despite this fact, no one knows if there was love between them. For the sake of both of them, we hope so. Otherwise, every sexual relationship would be tainted with bleak and mercenary nuances that, in the coldness of the aftermath, kill the Lucretian shudders of the "during," and the Peynet-ish or Hamiltonian (the photography of sensuality and flou) anxiety of the "before."

Nonetheless, Jefferson's story does not end here. Just consider Monticello, or even Jefferson's second home, the lesser-known Poplar Forest. This second home lies one hundred miles south of Charlottesville at the foot of the enchanting Blue Ridge Mountains, just a short distance from the spectral Lynchburg, a jungle of neo-something churches, seemingly deserted and surrounded by slums, located upon a steeply sloped hill. Poplar Forest, thanks to the efforts of volunteers, is gradually returning to the state it was in when it was Jefferson's second home, before a century-long odyssey of fires, negligence, and destruction. Visiting Jefferson's estates, the desire seizes you to return to that epoch and enter that world, that mentality, and in particular, the mind of that man of so many internal contradictions and ambiguities. Jefferson was a man of reticence and certainty, of strength and weakness, of shyness and audacity; all this and more wrapped up into one. Jefferson was an American Sphinx, who hid both in public and in private his uncertainties and insecurities behind a veil of silence—a lost sphinx, solemn and austere, deep in the heart of the Poplar Forest.

A boring film by James Ivory with Nick Nolte, who unfortunately was unable to grasp Jefferson's "Europeanicity," portrays his five years as ambassador in Paris. Instead, a long poem by Mary Jo Salter, distinguished contemporary American poet, titled "The Hand of Thomas Jefferson," splendidly describes Jefferson's internal struggle that began the moment his right hand penned the Declaration of Independence. From there, the hand then broke in Paris, ending his romance with the beautiful Maria Cosway (tragically, already married). It was the hand that wrote letters giving us Jefferson in his totality, much more so than public documents or the only book he ever completely wrote; and it was the hand that for many years caressed Sally's ebony body. Unfortunately, Ivory's film reached us and not Salter's poem or even Ellis's book, which, except for a *cul de sac* defending his Jeffersonian abstinence thesis, is still brilliant and keen.

The flood of writings that accompanied the multi-faceted 1993 festivities includes two texts by two great historians published by the Institute for Advanced Study at Princeton, unfortunately in an edition that is not available to the general public (*Two Lectures on Thomas Jefferson*, Princeton 1993). The first essay is by a 19th-century German historian, Peter Paret, expert, among other things, on Clausewitz, as well as on German liberalism. The second is by Bernard Bailyn, Harvard professor and one of the most important scholars on the political and ideological history of the American Revolution, along with Gordon Wood, professor at Brown (and author of a recently published book on American radicalism during the Revolution).

Paret addresses the core of Jefferson's thought, his being, and his heritage—liberalism. Inasmuch as one could define Jefferson's approach as "radical" for the historical context, we know that his liberalism had all the limits of a thinker influenced by early Enlightenment philosophers. He was more in line with Montesquieu and Rousseau than with Condorcet and other ideologues, and more akin to Locke than to Hume. Jefferson's liberalism has aristocratic tones, and his society of free men does not include all men, but only those whose status and ability (the fundamental dyad in the history of individual rights) resembled the revered roman *cives*. However, even among the *"cives americani,"* Jefferson was discriminatory with, for example, granting the right to vote.

Jefferson believed in a kind of "aristocracy" among free men, which excluded women, blacks, and even whites who did not fall within a certain financial class and education, at least in most cases. His model was the Greek system. In fact, his quandary concerned the liberty of the ancients, the comparison between Sparta and Athens (the more urbane French revolutionaries, following the steps of the American revolutionaries, also contemplated which one of the two was the best model to follow). For the most part, Jefferson appeared unprepared for the liberal 19th century idea that perfected the model set forth in the previous century. However, this model was subsequently confronted with the historical problem of application: the birth of the mass society, first in Europe and then America, created a considerable challenge to liberal thought, which was created for the few enjoying favorable social and economic conditions. Liberalism: this truly was the great conceptual knot with which Jefferson struggled.

During those fundamental years in Paris from 1784 to 1789, even without realizing what was underway (how many people at the time really understood and how far in advance?), overwhelmed by problems with his French, his daughter who wanted to become a nun, and his more or less platonic love story with the enchanting Cosway, Jefferson was nonetheless considered a prophet by the future Jacobins. They also consulted him, of course, about how to write a bill of rights. Jefferson's love for French culture, from the "high" culture of Rousseau, Voltaire, and Montesquieu (whom he adored to the extent of writing the introduction to the 19th century commentary by Destutt de Tracy on the *Esprit des Lois*), to his predilection for French wines, furniture, music, and cuisine, was checked by his horror for the inequalities in the reign of Louis XVI, with vast properties abandoned or set aside as hunting reserves for the nobility while the peasants died of hunger.

Perhaps the desolation and the poverty of the French countryside (as well as, although to a lesser degree, the Italian ones that he described in his travel diary) instilled in Jefferson that visceral love for social justice and equality which characterized him throughout the rest of his life. In fact, if one visits Monticello, one notes that the slaves' quarters enjoyed a certain degree of comfort unfathomable for slaves of nearby plantations, even if the structures and the amenities, when compared to today's standards, would disturb us. But if the horror of poverty, inequality, and the unfair distribution of land brought about repercussions in his political life, beginning with the laws on the distribution of property, as Bailyn masterly recounts, he was appalled by the decadence in which the court and the nobility languished. He described them as faithful disciples of de Sade, intent on betrayal and being betrayed, constructing fervent edifices to fill with ardent and bewigged bodies to disguise their algid and beastly souls. Jefferson the architect preferred the sober luxury of his neoclassicism, very British, with red brick and marble columns, that render Monticello, the University of Virginia's Charlottesville campus, and the remote Poplar Forest a delight to behold.

Above all, and this is fundamental to understanding the value of Jefferson's spiritual heritage, he set against Europe's promiscuity, vices, laziness and decadence the solid values of the now-emancipated colonies: the value attributed to a modest lifestyle, family, and hard work in a rugged country. A dual myth was born with Jefferson: that of European decadence and that of the vigor of the American frontier and American health, both moral and physical. A singular episode was his clash with Buffon, the famous naturalist who believed that the American land was comparatively young, and therefore its animals and plants smaller. Nothing could have been further from the truth, and Jefferson had elk and other animal skulls imported to contradict *ipso facto* the oracular Buffon. But despite Jefferson's admirable efforts, Buffon's theory continued to be influential all the way to Hegel—and to Hegel, Alexander von Humboldt specified with irony that the vast American fauna was not exactly *mignonne* as the great Swabian professor still thought. Jefferson applied the concept of vigor and purity also and above all to women, comparing the "Amazonian" libertine French women to the "angelic" women of the American hearth. These American women did not involve themselves with politics as the French women did and had the "common sense" (ah, the magical formula of Paine!) to place domestic happiness above all other forms. Decadence belonged to corrupt Europe, to that world divided into "states," to libertinism.

Myths are not easy to eradicate. In fact, they are still strong enough to shape a large part of the American mentality. This can be seen in the young American college women who come to Italy or France in search of a "libertine" adventure, but who mistakenly find themselves in the arms of Momma's boys afraid to even give them a kiss without parental permission (or, even worse, with those scoundrels who simply take advantage of them). Jefferson completely overlooked the fact that between "libertinism" and "liberalism" there is more than etymological assonance. In fact, it is not by mere chance that from the pen of liberal *par excellence* Benjamin Constant flowed his Adolphe, an intricate interplay between lover and libertine. Liberty, conceived as liberation from the constraints of the ancien regime and from the oppression of Catholic morality, implies a Promethean liberation, which, if it stirs up society in a positive manner through market creation and broadening horizons, simultaneously frees repressed individuality in myriad other areas. It is the vice and virtue of modern society. The first of the modern societies, Walpole's England, understood this: Mandeville's fascinating work *The Fable of the Bees* tells us as much, a half century before Jefferson's ascent.

Thus it is Jefferson who began the never-ending story of love and hate that has characterized the relationship between the United States and Europe. It is from this perspective that Jefferson's heritage should be understood, and it is from this primary contradiction and its nuances that all the other nuances can be read. The chapter that Ellis dedicates to Jefferson's "French" years begins with two quotes acutely chosen from Jefferson's epistolary. The first is from a letter dated August 18th, 1785, to Eliza House Trist:

I am much pleased with the people of this country. The roughness of the human mind are so thoroughly rubbed off with them that it seems as one might glide thro' a whole life among them without a justle.

However, less than a month later, he wrote to Baron Geismar, again from Paris:

I am savage enough to prefer the woods, and the independence of Monticello, to all the brilliant pleasure of this gay capital.

This is the beginning, then, of the fatal inferiority/superiority complex that ties the inhabitants of the New World to the Old one. In short, it is a European syndrome so extreme that Jefferson even violated the revolutionary embargo to have an excessively expensive piano shipped from England in order to furnish the hexagonal quarters of Monticello. Jefferson's relationship with Europe is fascinating. Paret, in his short 1993 volume attempting to create a parallel Plutarchian life, made an interesting comparison of Jefferson to Wilhelm von Humboldt, another great liberal thinker who perhaps was of greater stature. Jefferson was a man who could speak some French and British English, but nevertheless, rewrote in his limpid and passionate American.

In any event it is worth bearing in mind what Bailyn mentioned, in his golden little book: "The reputations of those who create the destiny of nations become themselves historical forces." For this reason, even when the DNA analysis is complete, we will never cease to speak for better or for worse, in one way or another, in one language or another, of this enigmatic sommelier of life and of politics. Jefferson was a truly American sphinx with too many secrets—or perhaps not even one.

III

On Knowledge, Learning and Understanding (people and places)

The USA are home to the most important, resourceful, influent, and welcoming research institutions in the world. While most of those institutions are related to sciences, some of them concentrate on humanities. I have been privileged, over decades, to be made temporary fellow of some of them. The following section, the third in the book, is divided into 8 chapters. Three of them, namely the first, the second and the third, are devoted to as many research institutions: the Institute for Advanced Study, in Princeton, New Jersey, a model for research institutions of this kind all over the world (the last scions: Freiburg in Germany, and the University of Notre Dame, which inaugurated its Institute for Advanced Study in 2010). It is the place where I have written this book, along with many other articles and essay, in 1998-1999. The second essay is on the John Carter Brown Library, in Providence, one of the major repositories of books on America published in Europe, from Columbus to the early nineteenth century. I have been working there on several occasions since 1994. Norman Fiering, who has been directing the JCB for over 20 years until his retirement in 2004, has made of this institution a model for humanistic research, not only in the USA. While I was writing this page, in December 2009, I heard the news that an entire college building in Providence has been named after Norman. He fully deserves this honor. The third essay is devoted to the Huntington in San Marino, California, a treasure both for botanists and scholars in literature and art. The third chapter, however, opens a less bright chapter in American learning. It is devoted to all the problems of high and middle school, addressed constantly, but never resolved, by scholars, educators, politicians, over more than half a century. Finally, other chapters are devoted to figures like Albert O. Hirschman, Eric Wolf, David S. Landes. Hirschman, a towering figure in many disciplines, most notably in political sciences, had a chair named after him in 1999. The chair was offered to Eric Maskin, who eventually won the Nobel Prize in Economics. Professor Wolf died in 1999, while David S. Landes published a most controversial book of world history in 1998. For their personality, and their work, they are all representative, to my understanding, of the intellectual and general atmosphere of the late 1990s. Finally, I devoted an essay to the 50th anniversary of Brandeis University. Its creation and evolution captures well the problems and challenges of America after WWII. In spite of the general crisis, which strongly affected Brandeis with the Madoff shock of 2008-9, the institution is surviving and still producing excellent learning and scholarship. In many ways, Brandeis is an example of the American dream, as it related to institutions (but after all, aren't institutions made by people?).

12

In the Enchanted Forest of Knowledge

The Institute for Advanced Study, a paradise of American academic research

The beginning of December was particularly pleasant in both New York and Philadelphia. A spring sun, not a hot summer one, and limpid skies shone over the trees and parks of the Princeton University campus. Groups of students and solitary joggers crossed the great battlefield where Washington's troops defeated the English redcoats two centuries ago; now it is a green stretch at the edge of state highway 206. Walking among the sober red brick buildings of the Institute for Advanced Study, an oasis in the anonymous and at times squalid state of New Jersey, one discovers squirrels, skunks, and deer amid amenable patches of woods. Following along the rim of the lake, I admired the modern library's edifice, cement and wood with huge and bright windows, pleasantly laid out across the campus green.

Wallace K. Harrison, the same architect who designed the United Nations building, conceived this library. Wood panels on the walls confer to the ambiance a vaguely Scandinavian flavor, while the use of mixed materials on the roof assures the right amount of natural and artificial light. Walking through acres and acres of green that belong to the Institute, one notices rare plants and trees that on this day are white and still, covered with snow. Albert Einstein walked with his cane these very same paths in contemplation.

The Institute for Advanced Study is unique in the world. It is a university without students. It hosts a small body of permanent researchers divided into two classes and schools: the humanistic one (history and social sciences) and the scientific one (mathematics and natural sciences). In a sense, the division reflects that of the *Scuola Normale Superiore di Pisa*, which has produced Institute scholars like the mathematician Enrico Bombieri, and has visitors *pro tempore*, such as myself. These permanent scholars are assisted every year by about a dozen young "members" who, while visiting the Institute, receive a stipend so that they can concentrate on their respective research throughout the academic year. The Institution is funded by private donations—considerably large gifts from people and foundations who want their name associated with an institution which hosted such luminaries as Einstein, von Neumann, and Oppenheimer. This is an institution that still welcomes scientists and historians of international caliber, from Irving Lavin to Stephen Adler, and from Michael Walzer to John Bahcall. Others include anthropologists like Clifford Geertz and economists like Albert Hirschman, a distinguished heir to the historical, economic, as well as humanistic tradition of pre-Nazi Germany—one of the greats that survived.

A group of friends of knowledge founded the Institute in 1930. Its creation was a singular event that occurred just after the collapse of Wall Street. A small number of New Jersey magnates led by Louis Bamberger, rather than trying to save their great fortunes (which had miraculously escaped disaster), invested tens of millions of dollars in research. According to these gentlemen, the Institute, and not just economic activity, would contribute to the rebirth of the country. Their foresight was correct.

I cannot imagine anything similar taking place in a country like Italy, where wealth is rigorously kept private for the pleasure and squander of future generations, and where the law does not encourage private donations to public institutions and universities. The Institute for Advanced Study truly constitutes a research paradise. Throughout the course of its seventy years, at least ten Nobel Prize winners have worked there. Certainly, its history is not devoid of crises and vicissitudes owing to strategic choices. It has also faced, at times, vindictiveness and academic battles for the choice of the *pauci electi* to elect to the body of permanent scholars. While it is nothing in comparison to the maliciousness of Italian academia, it is still powerful enough to instigate occasional scandals and heated public discussion, as Fred Inglis's recent biography of Clifford Geertz testifies.

In a way the Institute, especially its humanistic section, today is in search of its own identity. The sacred giants of the past who still stroll through its halls and the library, ripe in age and wisdom, are close to retiring or already emeritus, like Morton White, Peter Paret, and Christian Habicht. The Institute, a center of conservative American scholarship, seems to be hesitantly opening its doors to "Women's Studies" and other trendy subjects, but with caution. Its latest arrival, Professor Heinrich von Staden, studies Greek medicine and magic with skills worthy of the old school, beginning from the domination of language, both ancient and modern, and ending with all the care and sensitivity of both a philologist and a philosopher. Feminists responded with other weapons: they wanted to abolish the traditional symbol of the institute that encapsulates the neoclassical image of the *Nuda Veritas* with a mirror in one hand, holding hands with a scantily clad *Pulchritudo*. Together, they lean against a laurel tree. It seems that they find truth represented as a nude woman offensive. The debate is lively. As an admirer of Klimt and Bernini, as well as of the beauty of women in general, it is useless to state that I would prefer this established truth. But, who knows…

13

A Look Toward Europe

The John Carter Brown Library and its efforts to discover America's European past

It should be so obvious. However, the European origins of the United States of America and the individual states in South America are not fully recognized, although this would be to their benefit as well as to the benefit of the rest of the world. The American world becomes increasingly closed and proud of it, for a variety of reasons. Today, there are more foreigners researching the American world than there are Americans researching foreign ones. And when the American world does open itself up, it turns to research in improbable relationships rather than those tied to its European roots. For instance, studies and scholars of Chinese history are flourishing. Professorships in African history, anthropology, literature, and even philosophy are burgeoning. Has an African philosophy ever even existed? The European heritage of the United States is no longer felt so strongly that its origins need to be studied. Moreover, China, as a prospective market, seems to be more receptive than the European Union, which still has a vague political profile and an undefined purpose and contour. Engineers and blue-collar workers arrive in droves from India; from Russia, academics arrive in search of better positions.

Interestingly, however, Russian history is perceived in the U.S. as a part of Asian history rather than of European history. This is perhaps justifiable. The "Europeanization" of Russia had been attempted but not achieved until Peter the Great and Catherine II—that is not until the 18th century—and during the 20th century, the Soviet communist regime attempted and failed to "Russify" Europe.

The European past, its preservation, and its traditions are at risk in today's America. The third, fourth, and fifth generations of Italian immigrants have at this point forgotten their original language, which their parents barely knew. They are like the inhabitants of Poseidonia, who, in a famous poem by Kavafis, sadly forget Greek. Italian has become a language of "culture," and, unfortunately, many Italian Studies departments have suffered under fierce competition from French departments, which have a significantly larger number of students and scholars. This is difficult to fathom unless it is due to the allure of traditional Gallic grandeur. This state of affairs would be more understandable if it were the case in officially bilingual Canada, but certainly not in the United States, where the cultural impact of Italian immigrants is without doubt greater than that of the French.

It is therefore so pleasant to see flourishing in Rhode Island, one of the oldest colonies and currently the smallest state in the Union, a cultural institution unique in all of America, and perhaps in the world: the John Carter Brown Library. John Carter Brown, a merchant (also of slaves) in postcolonial New England, began acquiring books around 1840, intending to create the largest library in the world dedicated to North and South America in European culture during the first part of the Modern Age. He collected travel diaries, legal documents, political and geographic works, and every other type of book or magazine that directly or indirectly spoke about the New World, dating from the birth of the printing press, not too many years before the discovery of America, to the first years of the 19th century, when America asserted itself as an independent state and the first revolutions for liberty in Latin America occurred. This is a large segment, almost four centuries, of American history. Or, should we say, European history?

If geographically it was and still is a continent in and of itself— the drift had not yet completed its slow yet inexorable course—politically it was nothing more than a vast appendix to Europe. In 1901 the library, still relatively independent, was incorporated into prestigious Brown University, which rests in the quiet city of Providence, *nomen omen*, a short distance from Boston and also close to New York City. Norman Fiering, a historian of 18th-century American political thought and ethics, passionately oversees the collec-

A Look Toward Europe 75

tion. Under his direction, more than a decade long, the collections have been enriched and now cover a wide variety of fascinating topics: from the first Spanish and Portuguese chronicles to the first histories and folklore written by Native Americans, to the precious proto-anthropological work of Catholic missionaries (and subsequently Protestant ones as well), including Franciscans, Jesuits and even Puritans who traveled to the New World to evangelize but also to study native customs and languages.

There is no lack of cartographic material, which is presently the focus of intense pilgrimages by scholars now that historical cartography has become a fashionable field of study. There are numerous diaries, manuscripts, maritime law manuals, accounts of shipwrecks, and correspondence among merchants working on opposite sides of the Atlantic. Reports of Italian voyagers are not lacking and the edition of Columbus's writings and letters is in fact one of the focal points of the library's collection.

"Speak to the past and it will teach thee" is a quote on one of the walls of the huge neoclassical building that houses the collections. Open to the public and meticulously cared for by a small staff, the library was recently enriched by a permanent exhibition, the first in the history of library studies, dedicated to Simón Bolívar, the hero of the wars for Latin American independence.

The library also serves as a cultural center—a model that should be used in Italy—by organizing conferences and offering scholarships to researchers who intend to use the collections' 54,000 volumes, an enormous amount if one considers that the subject matter is quite narrow, even specialized. Twenty percent of the collection is comprised of books published before 1700. A series of small exhibitions of works from the permanent collection attracts a broad audience not limited to scholars, but also students and tourists. Often these are drawings and etchings of great interest, like the insects painted by the German naturalist Merian in the Dutch Antilles or the maps that describe, with assiduous illustrations, Virginia's virgin territories, where English colonists were the first to set foot at the beginning of the 17th century.

An exhibition on Jews and the New World has been planned for a long time. It will display, among other pieces, works of Jewish voyagers and geographers who wrote about this new continent in the first half of the modern age. These voyagers intuited that it was to become a sort of Promised Land, although, for the entire first half of the modern age, only a few ventured there, at least with respect to North America. Extraordinarily rich, on the other hand, is the history of the *marranos* who ventured into Latin America, leaving Spain and Portugal in search of a better life that they did not always find. Previous exhibitions have brilliantly documented the manner in which the Italians, the Scottish, and more recently the Dutch, arriving from their respective mother lands, related to this fascinating and dangerous new world, one which unexpectedly would become the most powerful nation in the world.

In these times in which economic and cultural globalization, coupled with the still uncertain contours of the European Union, have tended to relegate the Old World to a mere province on the intercontinental map of trade and knowledge, the John Carter Brown Library dedicates commendable energy to the protection of a heritage as immense as it is threatened. It reminds us that Europe was once much larger in every sense than it is today.

14

To School, for What?

Published and unpublished materials for a discussion regarding American elementary education

In the growing public debate over the changes in the Italian educational system, the American model is having a profound impact, both explicitly and implicitly. After the fall of the USSR, the United States has become the indisputable economic, political and militaristic leader of the modern world. Thus, it is no surprise that other industrialized nations would like to imitate certain aspects of the American system that seem to form the basis of such extraordinary success. Whether one wants to imitate the American educational system or not, for the sake of intelligent debate it is imperative to have an accurate idea, or at least as accurate and updated as possible, of the historical foundations as well as the current movements.

Chiara Nappi, professor of physics at the Institute for Advanced Study, made the following remark not because she had a particular interest in American schools or a sense of patriotic loyalty toward Italy—she has lived in the States for over ten years, leaving behind her beloved Naples to follow her husband, another renowned physicist—but because she was the mother of children who have attended American schools.

> In Italy, it is at times sufficient to write a thesis on the United States to be considered an Americanist. Such a thesis may eventually land on the benches of members of Parliament, who would cite examples (of course, with great caution—especially if a liberal) from the grand country of the Stars and Stripes to the *Bel Paese*.

Perhaps it is for this reason that Nappi had so much difficulty getting her essay on American elementary education published in Italy; it was a critical editorial with quite appropriate observations given that she raised children in the system. Perhaps it is just for this reason that she faced difficulty.

American high schools are in decline. At the beginning of the 1998-1998 academic year, a New York high school distributed a golden book of maxims on good behavior based upon a guide to European etiquette. Washington had copied this very same etiquette when he was an adolescent. In his unquenchable thirst for nobility and perfection, it served as his snobbish personal *viaticum* for his own future in society and, perhaps, for that of a society he imagined. He made out rather well. While Jefferson maligned Washington as a plain and stupid conservative, no one ever made any observations, neither *ante* nor *post mortem*, of the manner in which he addressed a woman or held a fork. I doubt, however, that today in public high school cafeterias or anywhere else there is any etiquette in passing a ketchup bottle. Perhaps it would have been better to pass out the handy golden pamphlet in the suburbs of Denver, where two bearded boys, with all the fine manners of renaissance men, entered their high school armed with weapons intent upon wreaking havoc because they felt "disrespected." With typical American obstinacy they did so, as we all well remember. Distributing Della Casa, Castiglione, or Guazzo, while at the same time allowing just about anyone to buy firearms, would be like trying to remedy an epidemic of cholera with aspirin. However, isolated cases are just that—isolated.

The problem with elementary education, of what to teach and how to teach, is widely acknowledged in America. On one side, due to low salaries and dangerous working conditions in degraded neighborhoods in which students enter the building through metal detectors, the number of teachers has dropped. In 1998-1999, New York imported about thirty math teachers from Austria, and while certainly excellent mathematicians, some of them could barely speak English.

Going back to Chiara Nappi's experience: above all else, it seems evident that the American system is profoundly unequal. Since state-mandated scholastic programs do not exist, schools create their own curriculum and are in strenuous competition with one another, mostly to attract future alumni and thereby future funding. Naturally, in the more affluent areas, the schools are much more elegant than in the impoverished ones. The same follows for the teachers, who are naturally better prepared in more affluent areas because they receive higher salaries and thus the competition to enter is greater. They are recruited based on personal merit rather than mega-state competitions as in Italy. As a consequence, only the privileged can afford to pay tens of thousands of dollars for tuition. (Keep in mind that this discussion is about elementary, middle and high school educations. For a university education one needs to at least double, if not triple, that tuition figure.) More than likely, these children come from families without the threat of deadly weapons or other difficult situations, and amid the various expenses of similar schools, assuredly, the expense of a metal detector is quite easily saved. Perhaps there may be one to "protect" the children, but surely not one intended to defend oneself from them.

While the gap between public and private universities is no longer so striking, the divide between public and private elementary, middle, and high schools is colossal, from quality to security to all the rest. One must examine exactly who teaches and what is taught in schools. As Nappi clearly stated, the teachers of middle and elementary schools do not go to universities, as do teachers in Italy; they go to teacher's colleges where they are not specifically taught a subject but are taught a *way* to teach subjects in general. But, if one does not thoroughly know the subject, how can one teach such a subject?

Nappi writes, "A student that wants to teach physics does not go to a university to study physics but goes to a college that teaches him the methodology of teaching physics." Thus, he knows truly little or nothing at all about physics. American teachers focus more on pedagogy than mathematics, and for the most part, they are not sufficiently prepared, especially in scientific material, on the didactic content that they teach. For example, a few years ago, a study of science teachers in American high schools found that a third of those questioned had never even taken a university course in the material they were teaching. Americans are well aware of this rather absurd state of affairs. Reviews are published periodically that update Americans on the status of the situation, like Linda Darling-Hammond's 1996 report that triggered outrage and infinite discussions which in the end were useless, as they did not result in any substantial changes. Another disconcerting incident was when a New York school district recently asked candidates for teaching positions to take the same general culture exam that students are required to pass to graduate, and nearly seventy-five percent of those candidates failed the exam. Thanks to local union protests, the exam was abolished.

Here enter the true lords of the American elementary school system: the unions. Their power is unmistakable and their protection of teachers borders on paranoia. Rather than scaling down union power, absolute local autonomy has paradoxically increased it. Often the unions find support in parent council groups, which meet with the regularity of a Swiss watch and the frequency of a heartbeat of a decathlon athlete. In a democratic country, all committees and subcommittees expect to have active roles within scholastic structures, much more than are probably necessary, and include such decisions as those regarding budget and curriculum. A fragmented democracy, in the end, creates a situation typical of *tot capita, tot sententiae*, rendering the entire system more convoluted. In the end, at school, one learns little or nothing at all, at least until the point in which one finishes high school and enters a university—at least for the minorities that do in fact enter. This is nothing in comparison to the great Italian traditions of classical and scientific high schools that are now demagogically placed in doubt. In the U.S., professors and teachers teach "how to learn." They teach their pupils how to have self-esteem and how to, in the Boy Scout tradition, respect one another. These are nice things that don't always turn out the way they should, and as Nappi observed, "the cultural relativism fashionable today and the qualm that content worthy of passing on exists find fertile ground in this environment."

Obviously, all of this poses the crucial question: What content is worth passing on? The answer lays in the individual's awareness, in one's sense of historical tradition and appreciation.

Objectively, there probably are no subjects in and of themselves worthy of passing down at the risk of foregoing others. Perhaps one could mirror classical or European culture but, in a world as culturally diverse as America, it does not really make much sense to use the European humanistic-scientific educational tradition. And what about the Indian tradition (of America and of India)? The Chinese? The Latin American? The African? It seems insane to apply an American model in Italy or in Europe where, when speaking about tradition, there already exists one *en faute de mieux*—Greek, Latin and Jewish. Is this perhaps not enough? The problem is global, and depends, ultimately, on political choices. Teaching how "to learn," to "express freely one's imagination," to "cultivate the imagination," and to "celebrate tolerance" is wonderful.

As far as the rich and the gifted are concerned, universities will attend to reinforcing conceptual gaps, which are by now old fashioned. However, the suspicion arises that beneath the refusal of pedagogical dogmatism and the unwillingness to teach weighty material like mathematical equations and literary classics, there lies a hypocritical laziness and underlining ignorance that unions foment to protect the scarce privileges of their members.

As I have already mentioned, Americans are well aware of all of this. In fact, in January 1999 President Clinton proposed that all entry-level teachers undergo a state exam. However, the unions felt that their liberty was threatened (the reversal of Tocqueville's dream: often liberty brings forth regression rather than progression) and subsequently squelched his initiative before it even began. When Nappi participated in parent council meetings, when she attempted to elevate the overall standard—and not as a snob motivated by the fact that she was a professor at the Institute for Advanced Study, but for the benefit of her son—she was immediately looked upon with suspicion, and not only because such a request came from a female European with a PhD in physics. Among the responses she received, one was particularly noteworthy: "You want to educate everyone. But tell me: who will pick up the garbage?" Nothing could be more class-conscious and obtuse, as if it were justified to deny anyone an education because he will *later* pick up garbage. And who could really ever know what a student *will* do? And even if an adolescent wanted to be a garbage man, is it truly democratic to deny him an education on such a basis? Here we are facing Leibniz's pre-established harmony in decidedly obtuse classist dressing.

Words are needed to render true liberals pallid, to make us mourn Giovanni Gentile and his revision of the Italian school system, which was mistakenly called fascist or class-based when, in reality, it had an uncommonly liberal spirit. One needs merely to consider the entrance to the prestigious *Liceo Classico*, indiscriminate to economic means but not to intellect. American schools have different problems than the Italian ones: bilingualism, for example. There are without doubt comparatively objective advantages to be taken from the American educational model—no salary is as low as that of an Italian teacher, who with a €1,000 per month pay would fall below the U.S. poverty line and thereby qualify for various types of subsidies. If Italy were to follow the American model, however, it would risk compounding the Italian weaknesses that many American schools do not have (funding, for instance), with those of American schools, such as the absolute prevalence of a pedagogical system void of content and the preponderance of suffocating parochialism. I would like to know how one "teaches" objectively without providing content. This seems to be no small feat. If there is something positive about Italy, it is its tradition of secondary education. And tradition counts for something, as is well understood in America, a country where placing signs like "since 1998" on restaurants and other establishments is important.

15

The Infinite Gardens of Mrs. and Mr. Huntington

A spring visit to Huntington Gardens in San Marino, California

It seems as if the great American patrons of the arts and science of the past two centuries, and also of this one, had and continue to have a predilection for gardens. As if gardens were a subliminal homage to nature surrounding them, American patrons tend to embellish their research centers with magical parks integrating a myriad of garden theories, from visual games with grass and water to labyrinthine paths amid a luxuriant green setting.

Such an example is the Museum of Pre-Columbian and Byzantine Art—the museum's theme is a conceptually strange coupling in itself—situated in the Georgian villa of Dumbarton Oaks. This museum is located on a quiet and reclusive Georgetown property that sits upon a small hill overlooking Washington D.C.'s flat panorama. Here is the famous center of Byzantine study, where diplomats and journalists are surrounded by splendid palatial gardens out of view of passers-by (a characteristic of Southern discretion, as Washington D.C., in reality, is a great Southern city). Built in the nineteen-thirties by philanthropy-minded millionaires, lovers of art and of empires past, the garden consists of nearly twenty different styles, round, or with fountains and ponds, and includes roses, century-old trees, colorful blooming flowers, insects, and small fish. In short, it is a true celebration for the senses, particularly in spring.

Nonetheless, in contrast to the relaxed and serene splendor of Dumbarton Oaks, the marvel that greets one's eyes on the other coast, just north of Los Angeles, leaves one breathless. Or perhaps one is inclined to shout to the heavens with joy, after leaving behind the frenetic crowd in the City of Angels and finding this oasis after a hot drive on the winding highway. In the heart of Pasadena, known to the world for the California Institute of Technology, in perpetual competition with Cambridge's famous MIT, cruising along sunny streets lined with millionaires' houses, one arrives at this little paradise known as Huntington Gardens. The gardens cover hundreds of acres, creating a little city within the city of San Marino, also the estate's original name before it was changed to Huntington. The estate originally belonged to a rich 19th-century family that named it in memory of their Italian ancestors who had immigrated from that tiny republic on the Adriatic coast between the towns of Pesaro and Forlì.

Henry Edwards Huntington did not represent the American ideal of the self-made man, for he was not born into poverty; however, in comparison to his status at birth, he died an immensely richer man. In an indirect way he therefore represents this American ideal. His fortune was due to his railway interests, which at the end of the 19th century connected, materially and morally, the extreme Wild West to the "civilized" east. The majority of financial successes in the 19th century involved transportation by land or by sea. Furthermore, Huntington also ventured into real estate investment in southern California—an investment still prudent today when everyone fears the "big one," the devastating quake that will split the San Andreas Fault and destroy the Eldorado. He married the widow of his uncle, Collis Huntington, who was even wealthier than he. Arabella was grim and bespectacled and, although past her prime, had one advantage—she was one of the wealthiest women in America.

More than they loved business, however, the Huntingtons loved fine art and gardens. At sixty Henry sold all of his stock, and together with Arabella and assisted by agents and representatives around the world, he began to purchase rare books, paintings, and even seeds. The palace of San Marino was already his, and he fashioned it according to his taste. Obviously, his architectonic style was neo-classic. The mausoleum, circular with external columns, commissioned while he was still alive, exemplifies his neo-classical predilection. The gardens were entrusted to one of the first landscape architects in American history, William Hertrich, who in 1904 began, at the age of twenty-six, a decades-long project, given the combined scope of the project and ambitions of his patron. In the meanwhile, Henry enriched his collections of art that, from the time of his marriage to Arabella to her death, followed by his in 1924, included almost every kind of precious object on the market, but with particular emphasis on the 18th century: English paintings, contemporary American paintings, and rare books and manuscripts from the Renaissance. Huntington also developed a section dedicated to science. Today, these collections constitute the Huntington Library, which offers about one hundred scholarships every year to scholars from around the world interested in utilizing the immense and rich collections.

Furthermore, not only the collections, which represent a *unicum* in California, in the United States, and in the world, but also the gardens can be numbered as one of the seven hypothetical wonders at the end of the millennium. Upon a stretch of land which weaves slightly among pleasant little hills, intertwined with large and small pathways, to the joy of its thousands of annual visitors, are a number of gardens. There is no obligatory itinerary. One can begin with the most exotic garden, namely the Japanese one. This garden has a furnished pagoda in its center and a small wooden bridge that extends over a lake in which there is a surfeit of colorful fish. Lion figures sit at the entrance in accordance with the Nipponese garden philosophy that visitors ought to concentrate on nature, or even better, to immerse themselves in it.

Of course, there is also the Zen garden, with its gravel raked in different directions to create a graphic design disturbed here with a circle and there with a quick horizontal strike. One or two huge stones sit in the center so that whoever may stop to contemplate can rest. From the Japanese garden, one moves onward, or backward, to the Australian garden, which, even in its abyssal difference, is still Oriental (for even if one finds it difficult to identify Australia with the "Orient," geography obliges us to do so). Here, one can stroll for a good half hour among the rich selection of plants, some of which are enormous. In total there are 25,000 plants that grow only in the ex-British penal colony, just a little smaller than the United States, Alaska excluded.

The greatest surprises are found in the Desert Garden. Here, spread across some fifteen acres of land, are enormous plants of every color and form from all over the world. There are cacti, agaves, aloes, and silk floss plants. Others of great variety are quite delicate and therefore hidden in the huge, torrid greenhouse. It all seems so natural that visitors are amazed (though grateful) not to see a rattlesnake emerge from behind these tangled, coiled, and stone-like plants. The flowers are an explosion of color and perfume, and everyone would be inclined to touch the stems, were it not, of course, for the inevitable task of having to remove perfidious thorns from his or her fingertips.

The sun beats down, notwithstanding the season. One leaves the desert garden with the satisfaction of having crossed through a long and varied path of plants "of names rarely used" as the Nobel Laureate for Poetry Eugenio Montale put it. Perhaps we share this disparagement with he who loved lemons, as his early poetry testifies, leaving other such plants to the laurelled poets. Putting aside Montale, however, the experience is unique.

Comfort is found in the small passageway under the rose paths and the Shakespearean garden. Unique is this botanical use of philology: cultivated in that garden are only plants that grew in England during Shakespeare's time. The visit ends at sunset; however, not even a week would be enough to explore all the gardens.

Among the other remarkable things is the fact that after the owners opened the gardens to the public in 1919, both private individuals and the government have continued to enhance the institution, which is already nearly perfect. In 1984, in a resplendent neo-classical building, the Virginia Steele Scott Gallery opened in memory of Mrs. Scott, great philanthropist and friend of the arts. The works in her collection are all quite admirable—above all, the 18th- and 19th-century American pieces, among which is a magnificent portrait of Sarah Jackson painted by John Singleton Copley. The opulence of her skin, the serenity of her gaze, and the air of understatement, notwithstanding her precious red garments, all represent a true archetype for the American matrons of future centuries (the portrait dates to 1765, when America was still an English colony, and would be for another twenty years). There are also more recent masterpieces like 1935's *The Long Leg* by Edward Hopper, an American marine prototype with an intensely blue ocean, the distinctive profile of a lighthouse, and the little sailboat that placidly sets sail for the West.

Departing from Huntington Gardens is more difficult than one would expect. Immersed once again in the hazy traffic on the Los Angeles highway connecting the desert to the sea, one immediately begins to dream of returning there soon.

16

Anthropology of Power: The Death of Eric R. Wolf

The passing of a great innovator not only of anthropology, but also of social history

Anthropology is a science that, despite Mauss, Levi-Strauss, and their schools, has always found an ideal home in the United States. There are many reasons: not only because of academic tradition, essentially inherited from England and Germany, but above all for the socio-political makeup of the country, open like no other to immigration from around the world, and at the same time traditionally imperialistic, to use a "loaded" but nonetheless inevitable word. There is, therefore, a double motive for the flourishing of American anthropology. To this one must add the relative novelty of anthropology as a discipline, and therefore its malleability in a new and vibrant environment, without an obsession to compare itself to the European model or tradition. Anthropology has traditionally moved in uncertain waters, and in the last decades it has also, fortunately, lost the character of study of "primitive" societies, its colonial and colonialist origin from the 18th and 19th centuries. Anthropology today increasingly contributes to and unites with sociology, scientific and intellectual history, and urban history.

To cite an example, there are winning anthropological studies of the highly civilized urban context, of the way in which diverse cultures and ethnicities unite and clash on the alien and apparently neutral terrain of large cities and their sprawling suburbs. In a fascinating book, anthropologist Micaela di Leonardo brilliantly describes the "multi-ethnicity" of Evanston, a cultured and affluent suburb of Chicago. Di Leonardo touches upon the history and the legends of American anthropology, especially of scholar Margaret

Mead, whom she demythologizes and contextualizes. But it is with the passing of Eric R. Wolf that a great innovator has left us, a scholar who will be mourned not only by his university, the City University of New York, but also by the entire world of humanistic academia. Wolf's work is not easy to summarize, especially as the conclusions taken from his research are among the most varied and fascinating.

Wolf, born of a Jewish family of the Sudet, escaped Nazism in 1942, following his father to New York. He was thirteen years old, and his secret dream was to study medicine and biology. By chance he entered an anthropology class and immediately fell in love with it. His academic career brought him from Illinois to Virginia, from Yale to Chicago. He spent nine years at Michigan, and finally came to the City University, where he became a full professor in 1972. His studies, not numerous but all influential, signaled a dynamic turning point in the concept of "culture," that great mysterious object, the *totem*, of anthropological research. Wolf conceived of anthropology as a science in which, secondarily but nonetheless meaningfully, concepts and perspectives converge from political, social, and intellectual history. Central was the fundamental notion of evolution, or at least "movement," to apply to those peoples that traditional anthropology, often out of comfort or laziness, has simply judged to be static, frozen in a long-forgotten time (in stark contrast to Europeans, in the perpetual motion of "progress"). In this sense, in order to understand the present, the study of "primitive" peoples, for example the aborigines of Australia, must take into account the possibility of development and internal evolution.

Wolf demonstrated that the divorce between anthropology and history is purely fictitious. His work, though completed on the other side of the ocean, should be seen as parallel to that done by the school of the Annales in France. In his first book, *Sons of the Shaking Earth* (1959), Wolf examined the evolution of Mexican popular culture; in an admirable introduction to the discipline *Anthropology* (1964), he shed light on the dynamic element of all those peoples erroneously conceived as "without history." The methodological cornerstones of his research did not exclude *a priori* any source or method, even at the risk of the eclectic. Eclecticism is traditionally the bearer, in the history of human thought, of extraordinary innovation.

A small book from 1966, *Peasants*, in remarkable anticipation of future historiographical paths such as "ecohistory," analyzed peasant classes worldwide. Wolf drew acute analogies, inevitable but nonetheless fascinating, between European and Chinese peasants, not only in their mode of maintenance and self-representation, but also in their conceptions of their lives, family, culture, religion, and (at times symbolic) power structures.

Certainly, however, 1982's *Europe and the People Without History* is Wolf's most celebrated work, and has been recently reprinted by the University of California Press with a new preface. It is an extraordinary book, dedicated to the impact of European colonization on the peoples of the New World, and to a concise comparison of the two cultures that met for the first time with such tragic results. The preface to the 1997 edition illuminates Wolf's path, and above all contains an articulate defense of the Marxist methodology and historical criticism that Wolf used, with great perspicacity and recognizing their limits, throughout his entire career. One cannot understand notions such as "culture" and "religion" without referring to economic categories such as the production world, and to political categories, such as the formation and the type of government and the administration of power. In this sense, Wolf is much different from anthropologists with a strictly "cultural" approach, like Clifford Geertz. And, even though the book is from 1982, it demonstrates the opening of perspective toward "World History," a discipline that is now becoming significant in American and other academic environments.

Wolf does not treat the relationship between Europeans and pre-Columbian peoples as a simple story of colonizers and colonized, but instead shows well the interaction and, when it exists, such as in the conception of power, the affinities between the two cultures. He also demonstrates how colonization occurred in a precise moment in the evolution of the pre-Columbian societies, and how it accelerated the end of those civilizations.

Wolf's last book is a fascinating voyage to societies and cultures that only a fertile and unprejudiced mind could have covered in the same book. *Envisioning Power* (1999) is, before a great book of historical anthropology or anthropological history, a manifesto in favor of free thought. It examines the structure and configuration of political power in three very different societies: Nazi Germany, of which Wolf had personal recollection, the Kwakiutl Indians of the Pacific Northwest of the United States and Canada, and the Aztecs in the century preceding the Spanish invasion. These are three societies inherently different and yet linked by their more or less predictable responses to economic, political, and social crises, which placed in doubt the continuation of the civilization.

Wolf describes masterfully how, in diverse structural levels, the culture of these societies created and adapted the dominant forms of authoritarian power. At the same time he explains how it was necessary for the elites in power to appeal to what Wolf terms the "cosmological element," or rather, a form of abstract, fantastical, and mythological legitimization of the authoritarian power, which creates myths (the annihilation of the Jews, ritual sacrifice) to legitimate itself and to establish a kind of "organic" cohesion linking it to the people. The elites, therefore, conquer and then maintain power by constructing myths drawn from traditions. From the people's forms of transmission of knowledge and religion, they manipulate the traditions for their own ends. At the same time the populace develops its own "mass" culture, based on the elites' distorted representations. But in the end both the elites and the masses are prey to the same destiny, subjugated to the same Marxist structural necessities of the society in crisis.

A reading of Wolf is illuminating. In a certain sense, anthropology was born in him, as in other immigrants, from the more or less conscious desire to cross once more one's spiritual and existential path and to examine power as a concept and practice when one has been personally banished or has fled from an immense and cruel power. Such is the case for Wolf, who fled the Nazi Sudet. During the war, Wolf interned near Liverpool and attended several lectures by Norbert Elias. From these lectures his interest in the question of power was born. And, as an American soldier, he returned in 1944 near his Austrian homeland to fight on the Tyrolese front.

And it was to the Tyrol, to the Val di Non, struck by his experience, that Wolf dedicated a book that is unfortunately little known, *The Hidden Frontier: Ecology and Ethnicity in an Alpine Valley*. The book is extremely important in understanding the Italian-German relationship and the life of the Tyrolese valleys, from the example of San Felice in Val di Non, where the local German dialect is the spoken language but the flag is Italian. Written with John W. Cole, *The Hidden Frontier* traces a socio-economic and cultural picture of San Felice and Tret, two minuscule towns in Val di Non, from their origins. Wolf and Cole demonstrate the reasons for the towns' often tense relationships with the Italian motherland, and together provide a surprising, and once again anticipatory, image of eco-history. They show how two towns just a few miles distant from one another speak two different languages, and in substance have little contact with each other. They have developed over the course of centuries two cultures that are often radically different. Reading *The Hidden Frontier* one understands much better not only the tensions in the South Tyrol and its aversion, in many cases, to Italy, but also, from a perspective that combines contemporary sociological data with accurate historical analysis, the many differences and peculiarities that comprise Italy. It is significant that this comes from a Central European scholar who has spent his entire career in the United States; it is also a clear invitation that an anthropologist makes to historians: to move out of the languages and countries in which they were born.

17

A Chair Named after Albert O. Hirschman

The campaign to name a department chair at Princeton in honor of a great economist and thinker

Now that he is over eighty, Albert Hirschman's infinitely sweet and intelligent blue eyes show a shadow of nostalgia for youth, and perhaps for his unique, inimitable life. With a step that retains his youthful suppleness, notwithstanding his snow-white locks atop a lithe and elegant body, Hirschman moves among the beloved buildings of the Institute for Advanced Study. The institute is permeated by the same serene sense of understatement typical of the scholars who keep it intellectually alive today at the start of this millennium.

Recently, a campaign has been launched to create a chair in economics in Hirschman's name, to which Deutsche Bank has already donated one million dollars, one-fifth of what is necessary. But for those who know his diverse works — his first relevant publication was in 1945; his last, a collection of essays in 1998 — the question comes to mind: what type of economist could occupy a chair with such a name? It is not merely a rhetorical question, due to Hirschman's intellectual greatness that is a *fait accompli* in the social sciences, and to the fact that Hirschman has been a truly unique example of multidisciplinary and interdisciplinary study, in his life as well as in his career. He, nevertheless, always maintained economics as his central focus. We may therefore reject *a priori* the most frequent accusation of being superficial and extraterritorial, directed to those who do not follow the canons of a discipline (or sub-discipline) in the great diversification-specialization present in the world today, academic and not.

Fortunately, thanks to the impassioned work of scholars such as Luca Meldolesi and others, Albert Hirschman is widely translated and known in Italy. On the other hand, it is in Italy that he graduated from the university, in 1938, in Trieste. It is also in Italy that he entered into contact with that great mind who, unfortunately, the fascists assassinated in 1944, the same year in which the partisans struck down Giovanni Gentile. In contrast to Gentile, however, Eugenio Colorni was only thirty-five years old when he was killed, and his production was limited. Some of his writings have recently been published, thanks to Meldolesi's vigilant care, while an almost complete collection of his works were published in 1975 with a preface by Norberto Bobbio. His few writings do not do justice to his fervid mind, which undoubtedly had considerable influence on the young Hirschman.

The Hirschman family is also linked to Italy through the story of love and political passion, which united Albert's older sister Ursula to one of the spiritual fathers of a united Europe, Altiero Spinelli. Ursula's memoirs, dedicated to Spinelli, have become part of the history of Europe. The human and intellectual circumstances of Albert Hirschman unfold in three continents: Europe, North America, and South America.

His life is marked by singular historical periods: childhood and adolescence in culturally fervid but economically exhausted Weimar Berlin, with studies at the prestigious French School of the Prussian capital; his escape in 1933 at age eighteen, during the tragic coincidence of the death of his father, an assimilated Jew; and the rise of Hitler, whom the young Albert had already concluded to be inauspicious not only for the Jews, but for Germany. From then until the end of the war, Hirschman's life included his admirable fight against fascism (he was a volunteer in the Spanish Civil War), and his intellectual development, a kind of unique *Bildung*, which recalls 18th century figures or political exiles of the 19th century such as Heine. Hirschman studied in France, then in England for a year at the London School of Economics, then in Italy, which he ultimately had to leave due to racial laws of 1938. Once again in France he dedicated himself to aiding the escape of antifascists to America, whether intellectuals or not. Until departing for the United States in 1941, he was in contact with other fervent antifascists such as young Franco Venturi, who had also fought in Spain.

The United States was to become his second homeland, but Hirschman returned to Europe in 1942 as an American soldier. Upon his return to the U.S. he worked in a group supporting the Marshall Plan from 1946 to 1952, only to then embark on another adventure. He became an economic consultant to the Colombian government from 1952 to 1956, followed with years as a private consultant. Returning once again to the United States, with his unique practical and theoretic experience, he became one of the greatest experts and most iconoclastic theorists of developmental economics. After several high-level academic posts at Yale, Columbia, and Harvard, in 1974 he became a permanent member of the newly established School of Social Sciences at the Institute for Advanced Study. Its first member was Clifford Geertz.

Here, in the almost enchanted quiet of the woods of Princeton, Hirschman continues to think, to work, and to be an indispensable resource to the young scholars who come from around the world. He dispenses wisdom along with his memories of a vast number of experiences and people, including Franco Venturi, the young, fellow antifascist adventurer in the Spanish Civil War of sixty years earlier.

The person who will hold the chair named in honor of Hirschman will have an immense responsibility, regardless of his or her specialty in the macro-discipline of economics -- the responsibility not to abandon the humanist element that characterized Hirschman's production from the beginning, and which has not lacked even in his most technical works, of which there are many. But the "human" and "humanist" side of political economics has been rewarded with the conferment of the Nobel Prize to Amartya Sen, who has always admired Albert Hirschman, even if at times criticizing his thought.

It is difficult to sketch Hirschman's intellectual portrait with few strokes. His most recent book, *Crossing Boundaries* (1998), contains three pieces of writing very different from one another. There is an elegy to convivial sociability as a form of precious elective democracy, based on the symposium of ancient Greece, a reconsideration of the Marshall Plan, and finally the English translation of an illuminating interview from years ago with Donzelli, Petrusewicz, and Rusconi. Hirschman's great ability, his unique character, has always meant having the courage to discuss common ground, the static formulations of political economics, and of politics *tout court*.

For this very reason Hirschman, an autodidact economist, fortunately cannot be placed in any one school of thought. Liberals would love to count him among their ranks, and it is true that a certain liberal and liberalistic spirit characterizes Hirschman's meticulous attention to the role of the state in economic processes. Perhaps this is a nod to his German birth, in a country that had been (and still was in a sense) a center of the cameral sciences, thanks to Weber, Sombart, and perhaps even Simmel. Hirschman's great lesson, among others, was that of always conceiving theories a *posteriori*, without systematic deduction, and without necessarily applying definite economics laws (in the manner of Keynes, but also Sraffa), if not to verify them empirically, or rather, a *posteriori*. Hirschman even recovered the value of truth (in many aspects indisputable) of Marxist economic analysis. His choices were singular and brave, such as the choice to pass from the Marshall Plan, which was certainly not without criticism, to the study of the economics of developing nations like those in Latin America; the affinity among the European countries that had arrested their development with the war, and the Latin American ones that instead desperately sought and continue to seek that development, is more than subtle. In a certain sense, the lack of something akin to the Marshall Plan for Latin America, substituted instead by a policy of onerous public loans, demonstrates once more that Hirschman's intelligent perspective traveled lands distant in appearance and geography only.

Certainly, Hirschman's interest and method rise above all toward potential rather than realization, and his lessons of productive heterodox and measured eclecticism benefit the global market. Unfortunately, this market—when subject to the control of the states—excludes too much of humanity from this process, and also tragically condemns it to constant economic regression and the threshold of total impoverishment, like the majority of the African continent, or Indonesia. As Fichte said, the philosophy that one chooses depends on the type of person one is—and, as Hirschman confessed in one of his numerous recent autobiographical revelations, his decision to study economics arose from the mass unemployment and disturbances in European politics that he had seen and lived in the 1930s. Clearly, this is something different from the economic-political *satietas* of contemporary America. Hirschman, therefore, is not a purely liberal economist, but maintains an acute perspective on the possibility of government intervention that can create incentives and is "assuring." Hirschman lies in a perfect but risky balance between the German school, state-centered, and the Chicago school, market-centered.

In his first large study on the international implication of foreign commerce, Hirschman had stigmatized imperialism that damaged poor nations while making rich nations even richer. Later, he developed the idea of collective interest that went beyond both the sum of individual interests and the false collectivism and true egoistic individuality represented by powerful nations. In works of intellectual history, like the splendid book *Passions and Interests* (1977), he revealed the ambivalence of the theoretical origin of capitalism. He saw in Adam Smith not only the initiator of classical political economics, as even Marx had claimed, but also the person who had limited the sphere of the discipline, shirking the authority on morality and partially on politics that was present in Smith's works prior to and less well-known than the *Wealth of Nations*.

Hirschman, therefore, even at the risk of severe criticism, has always tried to include "interests" and "passions" in equal measure, contrasting their divorce begun in the early modern age and completed, according to his analysis, during the Illuminist era. In the late 1980s, Hirschman's economic vision, not exclusively utilitarian or celebratory of pure "interest," found a notable echo in the work of economists such as Sen or Alessando Pizzorno. These economists began to investigate the "passionate" and not merely egoistical motives of economic decisions, and their theoretical repercussions in macroeconomics.

In all this, Hirschman maintained a coherent trust in the economic progress of nations. The title of one of his books, *Journeys Toward Progress*, dedicated to South American political economics, has something splendidly 18th century about it. At the same time, however, Hirschman diminishes the forecasting ability of the economist, in stark contrast with theorists such as Leontief. He always coupled empiricism to theory, comprehension not only of an object, but above all, of the way in which those interested in the object (for example in the case of politicians and economic leaders in Latin America) understood and viewed it. His general conclusions regarding developing nations, for example, according to the degree to which they experience tension between a wish to develop and resistance to change, could also be applied to countries like Italy, countries that are certainly not "developing," but that perhaps are not developed to their full potential.

As Meldolesi justifiably noted in a monograph on Hirschman, he moves with "sagacious naturalness" from psychology to anthropology, from politics to geography to social, economic, and intellectual history without ever losing sight of his economic and economic-political perspective, unlike many contemporary social scientists. Hirschman's humanistic vision is never exclusive; his reflection on the worth of the individual leads him to also consider that the way to measure a country's wealth lies not so much in the pro-capita earnings as in the fair distribution and progressive widening of wealth, even at the cost of temporarily sacrificing certain classes.

Equally, Hirschman distrusts a conception of the economy as following perfect, autonomous laws; he keeps well in mind the heteronymous element in economic decisions and developments—under the form of state, or "ideological," action. In fact, it is a foundation of his thought. If one considers the weight of Catholic ideology (far more so than Communism) in the development of the Italian economy, one cannot but agree with the German-American economist Hirschman's analysis regarding the fragility of democracy is equally interesting from the perspective of the Italian situation, especially regarding contemporary democracies, insomuch as they are bound to the complexity and imperfection of the deliberative process. After all, another great intuition of his, espoused in a work from 1986, is that a country's type of government depends enormously on its capacity to listen to differing opinions of its people, or to know everything in advance—the first nations will be inclined to democracy, the second toward a more authoritarian government.

Formulated differently and for reasons of space merely summarized here, Hirschman's thesis echoes and elaborates on Montesquieu, a classical thinker of the 18th century. Someone, therefore, taking the professorship named after Hirschman, will have in some way the responsibility of carrying on, if not his work—a *unicum* far too tied to a liberal and adventurous existence—then at least his spirit, which seems a job for Sisyphus. But it is also urgent in an America that is by now the only great world power that political economics finds a continuer of Hirschman who knows how to integrate a measured and panoramic view of the past with an enthusiastic and empirical contemplation of the present, case by case, region by region, according both to one's inclinations and to the current configuration of the world. This is such a world where, while great nations reach historical peaks of wealth and power, others such as Brazil and Indonesia are figuratively sinking. Entire continents such as Africa are drifting away without the West even noticing, much less thinking of offering any remedy.

In the infinitely wise blue eyes of the elderly Albert Hirschman, one notes myriad far worlds, thanks to him brought near. These include postwar Europe, Latin America in the 1950s, and also the magniloquent tradition of European thought that he knew how to wisely keep alive and adapt to a world in constant, dramatic change.

18

Brandeis at Fifty

**Brandeis University in Waltham celebrates
fifty years of education and tradition**

Like every great family, institution and dynasty, the recently founded Brandeis University in Waltham, Massachusetts, an industrial town on the outskirts of Boston, enjoys enveloping itself in an aura of traditions. As legend has it, in distant 1632, a few years after the founding of the Massachusetts Bay Colony, the governor of Massachusetts Bay climbed upon a high rock from which he could observe, brimming with promise, the increasing flow of traffic in the Boston port, which was still a small city having been founded just two years earlier. The rock was to become the exact point where ground would be broken for Brandeis University three centuries (and sixteen years) later.

In the fall of 1998 Brandeis celebrated its fiftieth birthday. Usually, most universities, particularly European ones, celebrate more ancient origins. For example, the nine hundred year celebration of the University of Bologna was memorable. This is not so much to recognize their past traditions, but so that they can use those traditions to launch into their futures, although in most cases this symbolic launch rarely translates into reality. Brandeis was born in silence, with Jewish capital but with absolutely no sectarian purpose, thanks to the New York Rabbi Israel Goldstein and the enthusiasm of a Jewish attorney from Boston, George Alpert. Fundraising began in 1946, and barely two years later the university opened its 100-acre campus, which had originally been home to a school of agriculture and animal sciences, the Middlesex School of Veterinary Medicine. The new university was named after a Jewish United States Supreme Court justice, Louis Dembitz Brandeis, who had distinguished himself in his fight for human rights and the moral rigor that defined his career and his life.

The nascent university did not aspire to overt competition with the prestigious Harvard University, just a few miles awa, endowed with incomparably greater means. However, more than a few of its founders did secretly desire to create a type of "Harvard for Jews," especially because of the reality that, even in 1948, many programs continued to discriminate against Jews and other non-WASPs.

There was also another reason to establish a Jewish-inspired university in Protestant, exceedingly Puritan New England, which had often overlooked lessons on religious tolerance espoused by Roger Williams during the middle of the 18th century. Boston is not New York. There were relatively few Jews and historically they were not well received. For this reason, the important centers of Jewish culture were traditionally concentrated elsewhere—not necessarily only in New York, where they teemed and where there was often fierce contrast among the orthodox, the ultra-orthodox, the reformist and the ultra-reformist, but also in more tolerant Philadelphia, California, and Ohio. Harvard, although it had among its professors the first Christian Jewish scholars (bear in mind that it was one of the few universities in America for many years), only in recent years has excelled in Jewish Studies. As Jonathan Sarna, director of the Department of Jewish Studies at Brandeis University, and one of the most esteemed scholars of Jewish Studies in North America, observes, notwithstanding Boston's shaky tradition with respect to religious tolerance, it represented fertile ground for a new secular university—even if it was inspired by Jewish principles. The history of the Jews in Boston has been one of slow but constant acceptance, in addition to being one of assimilation: Boston still represents the cultural center of the country, and traditionally Jews from all over the world have flocked there to study, often in disadvantaged conditions, in pursuit of their interpretation of the American dream: a degree conferred from a prestigious institution with the career possibilities that such a degree inevitably bestows.

American Jews studying in Boston increasingly attempt to accentuate their "American-ness," often at the expense of their Jewish origins. Justice Brandeis was not from Boston but he studied there, achieving excellence in his coursework before achieving the same excellence in his legal career. The university enjoyed its first fifty years of success characterized by a constant growth in terms of national and international recognition, quality of its faculty, and competitiveness of its students, even if among the voices of elation, some critical ones were heard like the one of the *New York Times* editorialist who claimed that Brandeis University's attempt to create a "Harvard for the Jews" failed.

In reality, the best Jewish students continue to attend Yale, Princeton, Brown and Harvard. To European eyes, Brandeis represents a form of the American dream, with the international growth of a university created from nothing, without state funding. It is often the case in America, while it is rare in Europe, and almost unheard of in Italy, that a formidable academic institution could be born from an idea or a dream.

Now, as at the beginning of Brandeis, there are many who believe in the notion of a small university—it does not exceed its enrollment of 4,000 students and 400 full-time faculty. The university, however, is at the beginning of a new and extraordinary tradition. Eleanor Roosevelt dedicated her time there as a lecturer with characteristic vigor, while Leonard Bernstein, beginning in 1948, taught music. In literature and humanities, personalities of great fascination and importance have taught at the institution, such as Frank E. Manuel and Ludwig Lewisohn, the former a distinguished historian and the latter an internationally renowned comparativist. In 1949, a year after its founding, among the list of visiting scholars from around the world were personalities of the caliber of Jacques Maritain, Margaret Mead, Martin Buber, and Paul Tillich—the best of Europe. From within the university, research centers were established, and not only in European and Jewish history. There were also museums, the most notable of which is the Rose Art Museum, funded by Louis Shapiro, the great Jewish art collector of Boston. The museum currently has a new director, Joseph Ketner, young but with a commendable list of credentials, who is enthusiastic about managing and increasing the most prestigious collection of contemporary art in New England.

The arts at Brandeis do not stop at museums. Brilliant poets such as W.H. Auden and Dylan Thomas have both taught there. Furthermore, in the visual arts, Arnold Häuser and Rudolf Arnheim have taught art history, and Jacob Lawrence, Frank Stella, Elaine de Kooning, and many others have taught fine art. In 1952, at the first graduation ceremony, 102 students received bachelor's degrees, and Eleanor Roosevelt gave the commemorative speech. In 1956, the architect Max Abramovitz designed the new campus—thirty-five new buildings that rendered the Waltham university complex solid, essential, and well distributed, void of classical or futuristic pretense. In the following years, the university created scientific research centers and international relationships, in particular, but not exclusively, with Israel. During the seventies, medical and biomedical research centers were founded that presently represent the *avant-garde* of American medical research.

In 1992, a center specializing in cognitive science and the study of interaction between men and machines was founded. In 1997, a private study discovered that Brandeis was one of the top eleven American universities that enjoyed constant expansion, and it placed the university as ninth among private universities with respect to research productivity. It is unique to Italian ears to hear someone discussing "growth" when making reference to a university, as if it were a private company with the necessity of profit. In fact, Brandeis is private just like most of the major American universities, and its growth indexes vary, but certainly they include an economic factor; however, scientific productivity is an equally, if not more important factor, which in the complacent European universities is too often not a priority.

One of the most formidable American Italianists, David Kertzer, who profoundly renovated 19th-century Italian studies and is currently a professor at Brown University, received his doctorate at Brandeis. Even in Hollywood there are producers who were trained in the industrial, perhaps anonymous, town of Waltham; Christie Hefner, chief executive officer of *Playboy*, is a Brandeis graduate. Certainly, the cost of a university like Brandies is high. In fact, two-thirds of students receive some form of financial aid, and the cost including housing and meal plan is comparable to that of the Ivy League schools, at about $30,000 a year.

In any case, statistics confirm that such an investment, over the long term, produces positive results: students graduating from the science and economic departments are the most requested in the

American market. And not all of the students are Jewish. A significant number come from all over the United States, many from all over the world. Brandeis, although it is young -- very young compared to the great American universities -- has already carved its place in history. Born under the auspices of Albert Einstein, like another glorious institution, the Hebrew University of Jerusalem, it has lived its dramatic moments. During the 1968 protests it was accused of belonging to the far left and of following cultural trends too closely. Nonetheless, it is incredible that a university born from the idea of a few men and which was given the name of a man of justice less than a half century ago has already reached such status. Amid the panorama of European universities, there is nothing comparable with the exceptions of Siegen and Bieldfeld, which nevertheless were founded with the support of the German State. Will such a situation ever be possible in Italy?

19

The Rich, the Poor, and David S. Landes

A history of the economic triumph of the Stars and Stripes

Julius Caesar wrote about himself in the third person, thus objectifying both the conquest of his immense power and himself, and leaving it to history to celebrate his name and the increased might of Rome. In an epoch of nearly equal luxuriance, the Renaissance princes and even the free republics (consider the annals of Caffaro and Giustiniani of Genoa, or the many Venetian and Dutch chroniclers) needed a literary, and above all, historical legitimization—a complement to the more or less direct celebrations of artists. The *Triumphs* of Mantegna exemplify such an artistic procedure, the service of art to power, one could say. And yet, it is often in this "service" that art reaches its highest peaks. With the intention of conferring immortality to the dynasty, the artist above all confers it to the work of art, and therefore to himself.

Civilizations that reach their apex, and even those only close to reaching their apex, need material signs, ostentatious, and at the same time assuring, of their incomparable wealth and unique virtue. Conversely, the historiographic consecration of the dynasty serves as an amulet against the possibilities of destruction in the course of history. In comparison to artistic celebration, it contains a positivistic element: history inasmuch as a "science" that recognizes itself as such, from Dilthey in 19th-century Germany to, above all, the great Marc Bloch of the 20th century (about which Carole Fink, an American scholar, has recently written an excellent biography), does not offer aesthetic legitimization. Instead, it offers the security, or the presumption, of science, which the powerful of the earth desperately need in order to legitimize their hegemony and to consolidate it over the masses. And yet the masses love beguilement by a historiography or philosophy of history (consider only Hegel) that places them within a winning state, under a successful ensign and leader of progress. This is the last stage of the progressive movement of humanity, perfect in its mechanisms, just as Hegel saw, *en gros*, the Prussian state at the time, which was all things considered still a province in the Europe of the early nineteenth century.

And yet it is indisputable that the United States, after the fall of the Soviet giant, and certainly even before, stood out on the summit of the world. Before Americans themselves say it, proud as they are of economic growth that has lasted for ten years, the indexes say it. These Apollonian indicators, so neutral and so terrible in their neutrality, assess the gross national product, pro capita income, pro capita spending, individual savings, and the prospects of growth. There is no doubt, the U.S. is the first. It is the land of perhaps the richest man of all time, Bill Gates, and a basketball player whose personal worth surpasses the gross national product of a nation such as Jordan. Ironically, the basketball star is Michael Jordan.

Therefore, if economists praise Clintonian liberal politics and the material conditions of wealth and developments with great objectivity (as much as is conceded by the science, when it is descriptive and not predictive), an economic historian, David S. Landes, may publish a tome of 650 pages dedicated to the *Wealth and Poverty of Nations*. The title recalls the far but always present model of the liberist and liberal Adam Smith (with the addition of "poverty" absent in the title of the epochal work of 1776), and the subtitle announces a question the response to which the reader will seek through the spatial-temporal excursions of the book: *Why some are so rich and some so poor?* It would be interesting to interpret the question also from the point of view of individuals that the nations in effect constitute. This question has already been posed, in different perspectives, by some historians and by many economists, and has resulted in more lucid, if less declamatory, analyses, such as the splendid book by Douglas C. North, *Institutions, Institutional Change and Economic Performance* of 1990.

David Landes' book was conceived and written over decades. Landes is not a historian of approximations. He writes infrequently, though he publishes ponderous works, such as *Bankers and Pashas* (1958), *Revolution in Time* (1983—in which he approached a theme dear to economic historians, from Carlo Cipolla to Eviatar Zerubavel: the invention and the revolution of the clock), and *The Unbound Prometheus*, on the impact of science and technology in Europe from 1750 to our time, a book rich with praise for the capitalist *ratio*. The book was published in 1969, the fateful year that witnessed the death of the greatest critic of such *ratio*, T. W. Adorno (certainly not loved by Landes) and the belated explosion of 1968 in Europe, a movement that did not look favorably upon the legitimist (for Western capitalism) theories of the Harvard historian.

Landes possesses a stentorian voice, makes himself heard at lectures and conferences throughout the world, teaches at the oldest and most prestigious American university, and is internationally known among economic historians. Both for the stature of the figure and for the powerfully Eurocentric thesis of the book, the work transcends the confines of academia. Of course, it is a book that is academically more than respectable. Landes knows how to present his material; he knows his trade well. The notes are dense but not overwhelming. The bibliography alone covers seventy pages, is in different languages, and would deserve to be reprinted separately; with some exceptions, one finds the best products of economic historiography of the last half century, and also before (Weber and Marx included).

Therefore, this is a book that praises the winners in the struggle of history and advises the losers. At its center lies a paean for (Western) Europe. He explores the discoveries and colonies first, then a sort of external revolution, then the industrial revolution, up until the culmination of European power in the 19th century. Inasmuch as he speaks little about America's triumphal destiny, Landes makes it known that he speaks *per speculum*; discussing Europe from 1500. In reality he sees the United States as Europe's direct descendent, reserving special treatment for pre- and post-industrial England, and such an affiliation seems even clearer. Before passing to a more detailed analysis of the book, it must be noted that it opens with a truly courageous declaration of war against "World History" (even if it comes from an emeritus professor that by now has no need to fear for his career, even without what the old John Kenneth Galbraith writes on the cover: "this [book] will establish David Landes as preeminent in his field and in his time"). It is worth citing the following passage, which surely left many a historian of the new (and old) world shocked and indignant:

My aim in writing this book is to do world history. Not, however, in the multicultural, anthropological sense of intrinsic parity: all peoples are equal and the historian tries to attend to them all. Rather, I thought to trace and understand the main stream of economic advance and modernization: how have we come to where and what we are, in the sense of making, getting, and spending. That goal allows for more focus and less coverage. Even so, this is a very big task, long in the preparing, and at best represents a first approximation.

Landes' *petitio benevolentiae* to call 650 pages a mere approximation is appropriate, given the vastness of the subject, the comprehension of the economic advancement, and modernization on a planetary scale, but the *captatio malevolentiae* of the first lines is surprising. Landes aligns himself against the spirit of "World History," or at least a certain part of it (and not only that part on the internet, against which he is so vehement, in particular against "h-world" of "h-net," a web site of Michigan State University that is not particularly relevant in the international historiographical panorama). Landes declares that he has neither anthropological nor multicultural pietas for the peoples that have "lost." The rich make history: to paraphrase Vico, the "rich" (instead of Vico's "men") have made this world. This is a bolt of political incorrectness.

Landes substitutes religious hierarchies with intellectual ones, and racial hierarchies—the Counterreformation, Enlightenment, 19th-century racism—with the hierarchy of economic success. In the American academic system where multiculturalism has gone from legitimate demand to totalitarian and totalizing fashion (especially in mid-level departments and certainly not at Harvard where Landes teaches—where they prefer hiring young scholars, a historian of African philosophy and one of German idealism, even if there is something fleeting about African philosophy, like Bulgarian music), Landes is not afraid to go against the current, exalting Europe, the liberal-capitalistic tradition, in sum the *winners* on the economic plane, of individual, collective, national, continental wealth. But, one could have two preliminary objections: one of greater relief, the other limited to the space and time of American academia.

Beginning with the second: are we sure that the departments that hire scholars of African philosophy, Bulgarian music, Burmese language, Samarian history, and Singhalese visual arts respect the demands of the new Empire, which wants specimens of all kinds in its rooms of wonders, academic and not? In truth, American and European history is studied regardless, and it is thanks to the winning Anglo-American tradition that the teaching panorama has now been widened to study even the history of the African middle ages (which was, in fact, a period of great civilization now lost, and it is a blessing that it is now being studied). The primary objection instead captures the spirit of Landes' work. From the point of view of money and success, it is indubitable that some nations must qualify as losers and others as winners. That does not mean that the society of the losers, of the "submerged," is of lesser interest that that of the "saved." In this sense, Landes seems too deterministic. His choler against multiculturalism does not hit its target; if one wants to study the history of capitalism, undoubtedly most of the world appears a loser, but in that case it is the chosen subject of the research, not history as teleological power, that requires the categorization in "winners" and "losers."

It is a very circumscribed perspective, legitimate but not exhaustive. Landes does not modify the vision of the past, he only better sets the contours of world economic evolution, better specifying why entire continents like Africa are tragically "behind" (though he never writes about South Africa, a singular case, or Morocco or Tunisia, unique even in their comparative backwardness). He also never addresses why great portions of Asia (in the ex-USSR) are on the brink of collapse. Landes has the particular point of view of an American of European origin. Adam Smith was not *absolutely* right, but he was regarding the *thema probandum* that he had posed. World history is described by Landes with extreme attention to detail and with a penchant for illuminating anecdotes at the end of each chapter (some are amusing, and spot-on, others less so: are we sure for example that the crisis of the English automotive industry is truly attributable to the apparently "natural" causes posed by Landes?). Even if he departs from liberal presuppositions, he risks becoming totalizing. "World History" is after all a great attempt to change perspective, and is much more liberal than the very liberal Landes. Every perspective, if it respects determined objective criteria of "science," is legitimate.

The doubt arises that Landes' work, in all its grandiosity and its indubitable usefulness, is an attack on attempts to change position, such as *Millennium* (1995) by the English historian Felipe Fernández-Armesto, in which an extraordinary attempt was made to view the history of the last thousand years of the Christian era from the perspective of an extraterrestrial: with surprising attention to moments and nations that are usually omitted from the history of the "winners," even if, in their own way, they were winners, not necessarily in economic or political terms. We do not live by bread alone. While Fernández-Armesto, for example, dwells on the extraordinary culture of medieval and modern China, to us practically unknown, Landes dedicates tens of pages to the colossus of billions of individuals in central Asia. It is a colossus that constitutes a marvel in the panorama of the nations of the world, for example the fact that China alone contains 21% of the world population on only 7% of the world's land. But Landes' sinological perspective is opposed to the admirable *curiositas* of Fernández-Armesto, or to the passionate depth of the great historian of Chinese science, the late Joseph Needham.

Landes demonstrates extraordinary parallels between European and Chinese history. In fact, he examines the chronological precedence of the great Asian empire in "inventing inventions," or rather, in creating the conditions for a potentially immense world supremacy: the printing press, gunpowder, and other discoveries. Equally, China began voyages of trade and exploration in the Pacific a century before the great European journeys of discovery. When Columbus landed at Hispaniola believing to have found a new route to the Indies, the travels of the Chinese had already finished. And yet, China's technological vanguard and its primacy in voyages of discovery and commerce were suffocated at their nascence. They did not lead to further progress and there was no speculative use of the technology and no development of travel, even if the trips were, in number and tonnage of ships, much greater than those of the Europeans.

For Landes the Chinese totalitarian regime had no interest in creating new markets, intent as it was to exploit its internal ones. Therefore, gunpowder, for example, was used much better by the Europeans who discovered it later. Printing in China was even stopped, and instead of contributing to knowledge, was conceived as an inert deposit of knowledge, since according to those in power, one could do without memory and active learning. The journeys were in reality great parades of Chinese power, with no true interest in establishing colonies and markets toward incremental development. They were only spectacles of luxury and might for the benefit and entertainment of curious people on the riverbanks. In short, the Chinese had enormous potential never realized. Europe, thanks to many factors, but above all to its fragmented distribution of power and the absence of a closed and despotic empire, began late but quickly surpassed China, which remained in its splendid isolation for centuries until the end of the 18th century with the opening of a British embassy. It was not until 1851 that a Chinese delegation arrived in Europe for the first World's Fair. But by then, it was too late. China was a static, often hungry empire, while Europe had constructed not one, but several empires.

History was set. With great defeat, China and Asia in general (with the Westernized and Westernizing exception of Japan) were destined to a perennial position in the background due to their incapacity and above all to the perverse immobility of their sovereigns. Is this the reactionary historiography of a cantor of *mirabilia* of triumphant capitalism in Europe, and therefore, in North America? Even if it were, there is nothing wrong here. Also from this perspective, Landes perhaps does not say anything new, but he also does not say anything blatantly incorrect. The transition to the East of the capitalistic production model of the West created Nipponese power. Certainly not this alone, but the production mode, the mentality, the religious devotion to work, the concept of honor and all the rest are endemic to the empire of the Rising Sun.

The Asian tigers are surely overestimated. Landes finished the book prior to the fall of 1998 (when it was released), when it became clear that Taiwan and company had grown too fast in the international markets. Japan has been recovering, slowly. But Europe and above all England, Germany, France, and the United States dominate the rest (Oceania still counts very little, a model of Western well-being linked to internal markets, interesting but not for Landes, who loves pioneers and colonists). Reading the book would make one feel proud of being European, even if the dollar has immediately obfuscated the euro, forcing it into an unpredicted parity. But these are only the sons that devour their fathers. The contrary is always better, with due respect to Dante's Count Ugolino. Europe was a primary motor of modernization and development in the last thousand years. Fernández-Armesto's vision in *Millennium*, intent on demonstrating the importance of the world's peripheries and of secondary perspectives, is in this way re-dimensioned, even if his challenge was precisely not to consider the concepts of modernization and development (if only, cautiously, intelligently and ironically, that of globalization) in his analysis of the last thousand years. And, on the other hand, Landes shows well from the beginning that his perspective is not obsolete. Among the greatest changes in the last quarter millennium, there is the disparity of wealth between the haves and the have-nots of the world. The relationship of the poorest (in pro capita earnings) to the richest could have been 1:5 250 years ago; now, in the case of Switzerland and Mozambique, for instance, it is 400 to 1. These are numbers worth reflecting upon and worth a ponderous tome.

Landes' book is articulated in 29 chapters, each followed by one or two shorter chapters analyzing in detail particular episodes that in some way demonstrate the thesis presented in the preceding chapter. One departs from "nature's inequalities" with a legitimate defense of the importance of geography in the context of social development, "yet it would be a mistake to see geography as destiny" –to arrive at a conclusive chapter, vaguely Kantian: "How did we get here? Where are we going?" The paean to Western society, to advanced capitalism, to the spirit of initiative and to liberal politics, concludes with biblical tones, and it is an actual verse from Deuteronomy 30:19, in which God tells man "I have set before thee life and death, the blessing and the curse; therefore choose life." Life, blood, and soul are all synonymous in the Old Testament, though Landes would also add money as well. And why would he not, as a scholar of world clock making, also place time as a synonym? But, alas, even flexible Hebrew won't allow it. (And, if he really wants to appeal to the authority of fathers, he could also reflect upon Isaiah, "he shall not multiply horses for himself," as a caveat to luxury and excess).

In any case, his thesis on the technological and sociopolitical prevalence of the Western model is inseparable from the moment in which one applies the values produced from that very prevalence as parameter with which to judge history and to believe there are winners and losers, in a Dantean way. But what if there were other parameters? If entire civilizations vindicated their right to *not* become wealthy, to *not* believe in progress, to live according to their own ideals, according to their "absence of history" (judged once again by Western parameters), and to paraphrase Eric Wolf? This is the problem.

The Western model risks imposing itself where it shouldn't. On the other hand, it is undeniable that the losers are by now truly lost, and the only model with which to save entire populations from socioeconomic and ecologic disaster is, in the end, with the disappearance of milder forms of society, the capitalist model.

Undoubtedly, Landes' book recalls the possible application to world economic history of Francis Fukuyama's theories on the end of history. Fukuyama's thesis predicted the "end of history" (understood as history of the great devastating events, certainly not the end of time, and as we know, time is the prime material of history) when all of the countries of the world will have reached a form of democratic government, essentially liberal and republican, typical of the United States of America. Landes corrects this theological, Hegelian vision, already advanced by the proto-Eurocrat philosopher Alexandre Kojève a half century ago, giving it historic weight: history continues precisely because a great number of countries refuse or are unable to radically assume the American model. Not also the disgraceful geography of the first chapter but also, and above all, political form condemns entire peoples to underdevelopment, even where there are natural resources. And politics is joined to the mentality of the weight of religious and sexual prohibitions, such as in Islamic countries, and the incapacity to create an honest ruling class in postcolonial Africa, which has returned to horrendous and bloody tribal battles like before colonialism, or even worse.

Landes' diagnosis is merciless, but it is also true. On the other hand, if well-being coincides with the Western lifestyle (and is not, to paraphrase Leibniz "one of the possible forms of well-being," but "the best of all possible well-being"), then the reasons that Landes cites for the lack of well-being in most of the world are correct. The problem is in his unilateralism, being a worthy perfector of master Adam Smith. Are economic and political liberalism really the only carriers of wealth? Perhaps in mass society, which is the world society of the past two centuries, they are, indubitably. If on the one hand the model of capitalist production needs the masses, on the other it serves their needs and satisfies, potentially, their desires, contributing above all in creating new desires.

Notwithstanding its inevitable lacunae, Landes' book is fascinating, loaded with thought and doctrine, healthily provocative. Other than with its fundamental approach, one may also disagree with certain points: is the world truly made up of "nation-states," or are there instead ethnic melting pots of varying nature, including the gigantic one in which Landes lives, the United States? Strange—but symptomatic of his positivist spirit—that Landes uses a typically 19th century notion, that of the nation-state, to define the states of today. His frequent recourse to fortune in order to explain economic success is suggestive. In fact, economic history cannot always have the pretense of scientific absoluteness in judging the past, and must also keep in mind the unpredictable variable *par excellence*, luck.

Even though he declares himself an enemy to anthropology, it is significant that at the end of a secular journey between successes and failures of states, empires, companies, and individuals, Landes solemnly states not only that the "law of supply and demand" remains the essential law of the economy, but that it is "culture" (not geography, natural resources, or political system) that profoundly conditions economic prosperity (in Western terms) of a country. Landes wrote, "If we learn anything from the history of economic development, it is that culture makes all the difference." This is an explicit homage to Max Weber. If beyond Weber, Landes had taken greater account of the lesson of Pareto, he would have been more cautious in judging the socio-economic ascendancy of the post-"Glorious Revolution" (1688) England in terms of the elevation of an entire, cohesive *nation*. In reality, it is known that it was an ascendancy only of the élite, coming from country nobility, the middle bourgeoisie (the gentry) and from the city bourgeoisie, supported by Walpole, and then also by the Tories. Therefore, perhaps this model is also applicable to other capitalist states. The entire nation is not always the supporter of economic advancement, though it is its direct protagonist. It also happens that part of a nation undergoes such a process and does not necessarily acquire wealth. This, in fact, is true for a great part of the world "colonized" by Europe. As the title of a recent book suggests, the arrival of Spanish colonists in South America brought about a true "holocaust," and the end to diverse empires and the destruction of entire civilizations. On a smaller scale, the aborigines of Tasmania disappeared in the span of roughly a half century from the arrival of the English. If Australia will become the America of the future, in the sense of promise of space and wealth, has yet to be seen.

Europe has produced a rapacious society, in the end much more so than "Eastern" societies of despots and "Levantine" absolutism that Europe has always denigrated, from the defeat of Xerxes onward. And also in his paean to the Western spirit, and the explosive meeting of avidity, technology, and politics, Landes does not cite more recent phenomena that are the last cry of advanced capitalism, like the internet, virtual markets, globalization, and all that which is rapidly transforming, once more, our way of life. But his aim was to write a history book that just touched upon contemporary life.

His perspectives are not exceptional. The poor will probably become poorer, and the rich richer, but Landes recognizes a moral duty of the latter group to the former, to alleviate their intolerable situation. But how? The poor must, volenti or nolenti, assume the way of the rich. They must adapt the capitalist system to their cultures when it is possible. And if it is not? But Landes, in his presumption, does not like compromises. If geography, the most immutable thing, is not destiny, then why should religion (Mohammed came millions of years after the deserts in which he preached and where he is generally adored), mentality, and culture be? If the Western model will continue to be winning, and inasmuch as "underdeveloped" societies are mass societies (and not shepherds in the desert, for instance), Landes is probably right.

Perhaps, with respect to utopian, disastrous, totalitarian, or millenarian alternatives, it is better that it is so. But then, it should be radically so: and let there be a return, perhaps, to colonial European Africa, if that would serve in saving millions of lives from hunger, misery, and AIDS.

IV

On Wars and Other Places (in peace)

This is the last section of the book, and it is divided into seven chapters. It also includes the least thematically coherent sections, for I deal with several subjects, seemingly unconnected. The first, the second, and the third deal with wars. Vietnam, WWII, and the Kosovo intervention (which eventually brought to the creation of the Kosovo state ten years later) were present in, or rather, haunting the American imagination (and active politics) in 1998-1999 no less than before. I witnessed the inauguration of the first "pedagogical" museum devoted to the Vietnam experience to be opened in the USA in New Jersey. A vibrant press and political campaign opened the path to the American intervention in former Yugoslavia, and the second chapter in this section deals with the artistic rendering of grief that followed the subsequent Kosovo bombing. The third of the "war chapters" deals with Hiroshima, a ghost never banished for good from the American consciousness. In this chapter I deal with a book bound to powerfully evoke that unpleasant ghost, *Hiroshima's Shadow*. History and historiography are the places where "never say never again" has an unceasing validity. Since cities, wars, and movies share more than a vague belonging to the realm of blooming imagination, the other chapters of this final section are devoted to movies (Spike Lee and Stanley Kubrick) and to cities (Atlantic City and Philadelphia). While Kubrick's last and uncertain movie, *Eyes Wide Shut*, captures a great portion of the ambiguities of the Europe-America relations, *Summer of Sam*, Lee's masterpiece, offers a clear and poignant view of America, of New York, inasmuch as it is an American city. Philadelphia and Atlantic City tell stories of decadence, pride, and resurgence, tinted with melancholy and occasionally tragedy that, at least to me, seem to capture the soul of America. They are a galaxy of cities, individuals, ideas, none resembling the other, although so apparently similar, so entangled in the same mighty lore.

20

Once Upon a Time there Was Vietnam

New Jersey's inauguration of the first "pedagogical" museum on the American experience in Vietnam

Boasting its modest bucolic quality, New Jersey license plates sport the motto the "Garden State." To be truthful, New Jersey is a huge garden filled with labyrinths, misleading paths, old train tracks, and dead-end roads, in which one could easily lose oneself, and often unwittingly does. While the dominant architectural style is neo-classical, it does give way a bit too often to modern-day strip malls, which frighteningly speckle the otherwise pleasant countryside replete with woods, small lakes, and meadows. New Jersey's eminently suburban character, when considered from a more ample perspective, appears to be one vast periphery of New York, and it coincides perfectly with the nature of its inhabitants: the upper-middle and upper classes, industrious as well as exclusive, elitist, and consumption-driven. Here, as Sheldon Garon, professor of history at Princeton points out, the Midwestern ideas of community and sociability are rare and precious commodities. The oasis of high culture which Princeton represents has hardly any interaction whatsoever with the rest of the state.

Even without Princeton's intellectual contribution, the Garden State recently celebrated a significant cultural and historical event: the inauguration of a museum dedicated to the Vietnam War, or the "American War," as the Vietnamese call it today. When driving along the heavily trafficked parkway (one of several) that divides New Jersey longitudinally, just after turning off of exit 116, a small green hill emerges in Holmdale County, and at its summit is the small museum. Its inauguration follows that of a memorial built three years earlier. The commemorative monument recognizing the American initiative is an amphitheater from whose center rises an oak tree, the symbol of peace and reconciliation. Of course, the memorial is smaller and humbler in respect to the colossal and celebrated one in Washington, D.C., a mecca for veterans, families, and tourists searching for a cherished name among the thousands inscribed on the funerary marbles.

PNC Bank, the private bank that financed most of the memorial, also built the museum using its own funds and private donations. There were, however, acrimonious polemics regarding the historical as well as political appropriateness of such an undertaking, and of housing the New Jersey Vietnam Era Educational Center in a cement cylinder.

The visitor has essentially three itineraries from which to choose. The first follows the internal walls of the cylinder, while the second runs along an internal circular hallway. The third itinerary is static: a room inside another, where there is a huge screen and benches. The educational function of the museum immediately appears as its primary purpose. "Neither celebrations, nor condemnations," museum director Kelly Lankau Watts explains. The museum's goal is merely to narrate what happened in Vietnam and in American during Vietnam, from the moment the U.S. began its military operations up to the present day, and it does this successfully. Images, commentary, and multimedia systems recount step by step, event by event, the inauspicious adventure. There is surprising attention given to the war's "pre-history," from the Chinese invasions during the Middle Ages to the famous 1771 revolt, a civil way in which a population, already lacerated into faction, rebelled cruelly against a feud between the two most powerful families of the country.

In spite of the director's word, one perceives a tacit condemnation of the French domination, especially of France's interest in acquiring at any expense, with complete disregard for the loss of human life, a balcony in the Orient from 1880 to the late 1950s. Documentation becomes more detailed the moment the United States enters the picture, claiming its French inheritance and supporting the South Vietnamese anticommunist faction with President Johnson in 1965. By 1967, the American death toll among the rice paddies and swamps of this inhospitable and decimated country was

13,000. A long wall of speakers recounts in detail the military operations of those years; the reactions in America and in the rest of the world; and the interlacing of everyday reality, war, social and political upheaval all in the frenetic years between 1967 and 1974, when the end of the Nixon era was presaged by the end of the Vietnam War one year earlier.

The heart of the exhibit is not only colored by massacre, napalm, torture, and execution, but it also narrates, with vivid imagery, the Hippies' 1967 Summer of Love in San Francisco, the assassinations of Martin Luther King, Jr. and Robert Kennedy in 1968, and political-musical demonstrations at Woodstock in August 1969.

Through its unobtrusive multimedia system, visitors discover a gallery of original and illuminating images. At the end of the circular itinerary—always ambiguous when dealing with history—visitors approach the exit. The section dedicated to April 30th, 1975, when Saigon falls and the North Vietnamese troops triumphantly enter the city eroded by corruption and war, almost causes one to breathe a sigh of relief. The cost of human life for Americans alone was unquestionably high—58,000 fatalities and 300,000 wounded. The exhibition documents the traumatic aftermath of the war: the problems of veterans, the mutilated, and the chronically ill stricken by the unforeseen side effects of Agent Orange. All this is known, but nevertheless, young Americans who often do not receive adequate historical training in school, not even regarding their own history, will, without doubt, appreciate the pedagogical tour.

The internal circular hallway hosts temporary exhibitions more closely connected to New Jersey's realities. There, one reads letters from soldiers who write from the war front on small blue pieces of paper that have a watermarked map of the Far East in the lower-left corner. These are not extraordinary stories; they simply recount the daily life of war, the private thoughts, deprivations, and fears. Corporal Terry Thompson writes to his family on May 1, 1968, "All quiet on the Far Eastern front." Standing next to me, a middle-aged woman in a sweat suit with almost yellow blond hair has tears in her eyes. These letters, images, and voices do not send the same message to everyone.

When the walk through the circle is complete there only remains the exit, and before going out into the pouring rain, I give a final glance to the two citations that introduce the exhibition. One is by John Quincy Adams from 1821: "America goes not abroad in search of monsters to destroy." His words are followed by President Harry Truman's: "It must be the policy of the United States to support free peoples who are resisting attempted subjugation by armed minorities or by outside pressures."

I compliment Lankau Watts for her choice; pedagogically, for the open neutrality of these two reflections and of the apparent contradiction within. History, I'm afraid, will continue to teach, and who knows for how long, that the contradictions of the American spirit tend to be so destructive that, in reality, one hopes that ultimately one of the two possible courses expressed above will be adopted that sustains the radiant eloquence of the Stars and Stripes.

21

Caravaggio in the Balkans

The "invention" of suffering in Kosovo in the pages of the *New York Times*

A reading of the *New York Times*, especially the Saturday and Sunday editions, is a rite that can occupy an entire week. The paper is so dense with supplements, sections, and advertisements, that in the end even carrying around the Sunday edition presents a notable problem. A reading of the *New York Times*, perhaps the most celebrated newspaper in the world, often reveals singular surprises. This is not only because I noted, with a certain bitterness, that in all that printed paper there is little space dedicated to Europe and practically nothing to Italy. The recent (1998) fall of the Italian government did not draw the attention I would have expected, and other events from home, perhaps irrelevant to Italians, attracted much more press. Above all, however, there are articles that elicit reflection more on the way in which they are constructed than on what they say.

An article on the war in Kosovo from October 29, 1998, captured the attention of our microcosm of historians, who from the enchanted forest of Princeton could observe the devastation in the Balkans much like the United States now observes most of the world: as witnesses of a shipwreck, like Lucretius writes, watching from the safety of their fertile shores. Its attention to the events in the Balkans distinguishes the *New York Times*, from the moment in which NATO armed forces, or perhaps just the United States as a single nation, were ready to enter the scene.

It is bitterly stupefying that once again Western Europe, with Kosovo as its neighbor, must avail itself of American force to challenge Serbian arrogance and cruelty. The European Union, or whoever represents it, should re-read Machiavelli, or at least a summary of his thought. To govern well, the Florentine secretary said, essentially two things are necessary: good laws and good weapons. It is embarrassing that Europe is capable of making laws at home, but, for the weapons, must cross the ocean. But it is not of this that I wish to speak. The five-column piece in the *NYT* is accompanied by a color photograph by Alan Chin representing the ritual weeping of a group of Kosovan women surrounding the body of Ali Paqarizi, a young man killed by a booby trap abandoned by the governing police.

Now, to an eye even only vaguely accustomed to Italian and European Renaissance art, Chin's perfect photograph must bring to mind the grieving figures of Caravaggio, prey to the ecstasy of their pain. Claudia Swan, a young art historian in Chicago, duly reveals the Caravaggio-esque elements of the photograph: around the two central figures is the body of the son under a red and white sheet, with only the pale blue face visible, and the mother who cries, half collapsed on the cadaver. The other figures extend geometrically from them, desperate, crying women, with their heads covered by white kerchiefs, their hands contracted in paint or spread, as in the case of the oldest woman, over the face of the cadaver.

The pious, wrinkled, yet lively hands of the elderly woman cover the face of the young man, smooth and youthful but frozen in absence of life. In the background, in the style of Caravaggio, is a yellowish wall, uniform and flat, on which painful humanity runs as if on the indifferent tape of history. So, Swan's mind brings us to the most natural interpretation and also makes us think, thanks to the placement of the image of the deposition, of Christ, where the Madonna experienced the redemption of sin by traversing the mortal, yet vivifying, suffering of the Son.

We are by now in the territory of art: *The Deposition* at the Prado, by Roger van der Weyden, is a work from 1435 that signals the beginning of the burgeoning of Dutch religious painting. Or, as Princeton art historian Jack Freiberg suggests, one can consider the European Caravaggisti such as Simon Vouet, who utilized the tragic play of shadow and light, the squalor of the background, and the scream of paint that washes over the mute canvas. And yet, it is an image that would like to, or perhaps should, evoke above all the pain of a real family and involve the American people in the suffering of an entire people, suffocated in its desire for freedom.

The article by Mike O'Connor follows the same path as the picture. O'Connor describes, with anthropological precision, Ali Paqarizi's funeral, and the hierarchy of family, clan, and Muslim clerics in the procession. A short piece juxtaposed with the article mentions that NATO could always bomb the Serbs. Americans, after having read the article but above all after having been seized by the perfection of the accompanying image, would not be displeased. But another thing struck our small group of historians about Chin's image: the fact that we have already seen it. Thus begins impassioned electronic and paper research until our impression is triumphantly confirmed. It is not Caravaggio or De La Tour, but another photographer, the Frenchman Georges Mérillion, who captured a similar scene of grief. The body is another, the name another, the family another, but we are still in Kosovo in 1991. Or, one might say, we are still amongst contemporary Caravaggisti.

Mérillon's photograph is even more suggestive, the play of shadow and pastel colors more subtle, the geometry of the faces more articulated and yearning. Caravaggio would have preferred him to Chin as a disciple. With this photograph, Mérillon won the World Press Prize of 1991. What does all this mean? That Chin's photograph was constructed in a lab, like the American-Albanian War in the genial film *Wag the Dog*, with Robert De Niro and Dustin Hoffman? That both of the photographs are false? It could never be proven.

They may be real. At a certain point art imitated life, then modernity inverted the terms, from D'Annunzio to Gozzano. Or perhaps art constructs life, to then make believe that it truly is so, and to therefore deny itself as art. Art invents emotion, ignoring that in the end the emotion that it represents is exactly like that, even if it could not be painted in this splendid way. *New York Times* readers will perhaps end up loving Caravaggio more, even though they will surely suffer more, up to calling for hunting and battleships, for the fate of the rebel peoples of Kosovo. Perhaps these people were innocent models for Caravaggio's last pupils. They were innocent victims of war and of art, for which the funeral and ritual weeping of Kosovo will become topical, like a deposition at the Prado: a *genre*, even.

But Americans know that if the Crucifixion was left un-avenged, it was only because their army didn't yet exist. Now, NATO may offer redemption, with the grandiose, Apollonian efficiency of its missiles, perfect like the photos by these last followers of Caravaggio, precise and absolute like grief ought to be, in order to be understood.

The one and the other, true works of art.

22

In Hiroshima's Shadow

A book that poignantly evokes the explosion of the atomic bomb, and the absence of fifty-year anniversary celebrations in 1995

History, it is said, is not made with "ifs" and "maybes." If Hitler had won the war, if the atomic bomb had not been dropped, are premises that usually lead nowhere. Technically they are called counterfactuals. At times, however, it is possible to extract useful results from such counterfactuals, and in 1993 the Nobel Prize for Economics was awarded to two American historians who brilliantly applied counterfactual propositions to American economic history of the last century. One of the historians, Robert W. Fogel, had successfully applied cliometrics to American economic history, in particular to the history of railways and of slavery; the other, Douglas C. North, had studied the relationship between political and economic institutions, producing texts that have become classics in political economics.

In all probability, if the atomic bomb had not been dropped on Hiroshima on August 6, 1945, and on Nagasaki three days later, the war would have continued for quite some time. Or, again, in all probability, it would have ended relatively quickly in any event, as was recently demonstrated, amongst several other interesting issues, in the profound, passionate and fascinating book *Hiroshima's Shadow: Writings on the Denial of History and the Smithsonian Controversy* (1998, The Pamphleteer's Press). It is a collection of essays and testimonials edited by two journalists, Kai Bird and Lawrence Lifschultz.

The book is a collection of statements and writings from six Nobel Prize winners, writers, politicians, eyewitnesses, and commentators over the course of fifty years. The preface was written by the formidable physicist Joseph Rotblat, the only member of the Manhattan Project, the scientific project on the use of the atomic bomb for bellicose purposes, to resign from the project and to have publicly condemned the bomb and nuclear politics. His was a lifelong effort crowned with the Nobel Peace Prize in 1995, the year of the controversial fiftieth celebration of its use. A book rich in content from Albert Camus to Albert Einstein, from Reinhold Niebuhr to Kenzaburo Oè, and from John Rawls to Bertrand Russell, it features philosophers, writers, scientists, victims and observers. There are previously unpublished accounts, horrific even if they reveal that which the world already knows. Eloquent photographs by Yosuke Yamahata capture the iciness of death and the stunned looks of desperation that followed the fireworks created by the explosion. There is the story of Shuntaro Hida, a young army doctor stationed at Hiroshima whose life was saved by sheer chance (he had a medical emergency out of town on the night between August 5 and 6). Dense with horror and disbelief, his story is a great literary contribution, even more so than historical.

From a village on the river Ohta, Shuntaro sees Hiroshima in the distance on a beautiful sunbathed day. He observes a B-29 American plane slowly flying across Hiroshima's skyline, not knowing that it is the *Enola Gay*, ready to drop a 12-kiloton atomic bomb. The B-29 releases the bomb, but Shuntaro does not see it. Attached to a parachute, the bomb placidly drops, almost as if enjoying its slow descent to the detonation point at about 600 meters above the city. In the few seconds following that fateful 8:16 a.m., 83,000 people die and 53,000 are wounded while 40 square kilometers of the city's infrastructure disintegrates. A blinding light strikes Shuntaro. Before he hears the roar of the explosion, before he sees it, an entire city will have dissolved, as in a nightmare, in what afterwards will be known as *kinko gumo*, "the mushroom cloud." The rush of air from the explosion lifts Shuntaro, and it sends him flying back for a good ten meters against a wall, covered in mud and exhausted.

From that moment, his life as a man and as a doctor is forever changed. For days he will encounter a humanity that has been reduced to a thing, men burned alive yet still breathing, their only clothing their petrified skin mixed with blood, huddled night after night in tragic, desperate, screaming and agonizing clusters around the once peaceful and pleasant villages along the Ohta river valley. For days Hiroshima, or what remains of Hiroshima, is in flames. And its inhabitants, or what remains of them, wounded and contaminated, roam like zombies amid the dust and ruins, in search of improbable escape routes, water springs, or a less cruel death. Reading the book, one discovers that behind the dropping of the bomb there were contradictory calculations regarding the number of deaths that would have been necessary to defeat Japan *if* the bomb had not been dropped. Truman estimated that it would have been necessary to invade Japan, with the loss of lives amounting to at least 500,000 Americans. Churchill exaggerated the figures, increasing them to 1,200,000 lives. However, military analysts maintained that the allied forces death toll would not exceed 45,000 and in all probability would have been even less. In any case, Hiroshima and Nagasaki were to have served not only to end the war—and Hirohito publicly surrendered a few days after the bombings—but as a deterrent to the Soviet Union, as relations with it were already precarious. Hawkish and reactionary generals such as General Leslie Groves were clearly responsible for the pressures to rush atomic testing, especially the July 16 test.

Certainly, if at the end of 1944 Nazi Germany had not abandoned its atomic bomb testing, and if they had built one, I do not think they would have avoided its use -- they would have used it extensively. Nonetheless, Japan was by then already destined for surrender. Many saw the bomb as a *coup de grace* that could have been avoided. Fifty years later the Smithsonian Institution would have liked to mark the event by exhibiting that B-29 bomber with the curious name *Enola Gay* in its grand halls in Washington, D.C. This proposal, however, created such an outcry that the museum's director Martin Harwitt was forced to resign, and in the end there was no commemoration. In point of fact, the accusations were that those who sought to have the exhibition really wanted to cast a gray cloud over America, by displaying the plane and painstakingly recounting the entire episode in order to condemn American imperialism and cynicism. That the Smithsonian could have had such intent is difficult to believe.

Hiroshima's Shadow helps to reflect not only that summer morning of 1945, but also the significance of the use of nuclear weapons. It is not an eminently historic or academic topic. Thousands of bombs are perhaps drifting around the ex-Soviet empire, like *ronin*, Samurais without a lord. These are the much more powerful heirs of the Hiroshima bomb. It is something worth thinking about.

23

The Beautiful Summer of Son of Sam

A splendid film by Spike Lee recalls
New York's 1977 summer of terror

It is common knowledge that dog is man's best friend. American bookstores abound with books that discuss how to raise, nurture, and help these diverse and loyal four-legged friends. There are treatises in every form and shape, in color and in black and white, on various species of dogs. The *New York Times* reviewed with great enthusiasm the paperback edition of a literary "classic" in the canine field (even though it had been released as a hardcover just one year earlier), called *Pack of Two: The Intricate Bond Between People and Dogs*, by Caroline Knapp. Knapp's book speaks of the great affection that she has for a lovable mixed breed, commenting on "the power of dogs to open up the human heart." Perhaps to the disapproval of dog lovers, but to the unanimous approval of film lovers, Spike Lee tells us a different story.

He reproduces on film the events of that muggy New York summer, during which a twenty-four-year-old psychopathic mailman, David Berkowitz, took a .44 magnum and gunned down six people, gravely injuring seven more. The police were able to arrest him through his license plate number. During the trial, with an irritating half smile on his lips, Berkowitz calmly confessed to his crimes. He attributed his actions to orders given to him by a black Labrador retriever that belonged to his neighbor, Sam. From this we get his pseudonym, "Son of Sam." Exactly twenty-two years after the start of that bloody summer, Spike Lee made a film that stirred up debate even before its release in theaters. The film is not an exposition on Sam, but on the summer of Sam: a summer, a year, a period of time in which folly in one form or another wafted through the air of American and European cities. On this topic Lee says a great deal, much more than he says on the Son of Sam, the mechanisms of mental deviation, criminal anthropology, or the *modus operandi* of criminals.

The achievements of Son of Sam were anything but great. In the film, he is described without glamour and keeps a low profile for a serial killer, especially for the police, for whom Lee does not spare any irony. At one point one of the investigators says on television, with extreme regret, "We know he lives somewhere, he must live in an apartment, an attic, a cellar, a loft, anyhow we know he lives in such a place." Son of Sam, in fact, is not even the protagonist of the film. The first protagonist is New York, not posh Manhattan, but the Bronx, Queens, and Brooklyn—places filled with ordinary people, where Berkowitz, in order not to abandon his social class (craziness respects the social classes?) kills.

The other protagonists are a group of young Italian Americans from the Bronx, on which the plot focuses. There is a young couple in marital crisis (a superb Mira Sorvino and wonderful John Leguizamo, who comes out of the marsh of "evil" where Brian De Palma's *Carlito's Way* had relegated him), who go from nightclub to nightclub looking for reasons and pretenses to renew their bad relationship. They finally wind up in a club called Plato's Retreat, where the patrons engage in group sex with great dissatisfaction for both; she is a devout Catholic, he is a macho male. Both of them share outlooks and expectations that are definitely provincial for cosmopolitan New York. Then there is the assumed homosexual who traipses around in punk dress—because 1977 is also the year of the punk. It is very British (from this we get the British flag t-shirt that an adolescent adorns in the first scene) in contrast to John Travolta, who had just exploded on the scene. Naturally there is the beautiful girl who drops everything to save him, and together they sing and dance to punk music and sell themselves in limited-distribution porn films. There is the collection of grownups with many sons and daughters who act like teenagers, and of course drug dealers as well, to supplement their salaries as waiters, bartenders, barbers, and drivers, when not unemployed. There is also a marvelous Lino Ventura in an important cameo appearance as a plumber turned boss of the neighborhood, to whom the police desperately turn for help in the search of ineffable, but pernicious "Sam."

Within this group, fear of the monster that has brushed by but has not hit any of them is ubiquitous. From this absurd psychosis, from ignorance to stupidity, the one who will pay the price is the freak of all freaks, the one who is the most different from them all: the young punk. After some indulge an unfounded suspicion that the killer is among them, his own peers will accuse him of being the monster to exorcize their fear (little delinquents yes, but assassins no).

The "beautiful summer" of 1977. Vietnam starts to be a thing of the past, like a bad dream. The heat explodes; it is one of the hottest summers of the century, with temperatures reaching over 100 degrees Fahrenheit. Disco music explodes. It is, in fact, another protagonist of the film. Elvis dies. His death signals a changing of the guard. One of the opening scenes depicts two young women chatting in a car, late at night. They are listening to Abba's snappy, sappy *Dancing Queen*. The killer approaches, the music quickly lowers, he fires several shots, killing the women, and leaves. In a few seconds the music returns as before, as if those shots were but a momentary interruption in a summer of folly, sex, and dance—and also, of course, death. It seemed as if parents were more afraid than their children, who continued to stay out late and have a good time, in a summer which was all things considered happy, in which once danced to Chic, but also to the Who, Grace Jones, and Peter Brown.

Now this all seems to be a part of history, even though only little more than twenty years have passed, though Travolta has made a comeback in the U.S., and Grace Jones in Europe. But the Who, the Machine, Abba, and other mythical groups like the Emotions are no more. Young people don't know anything about them; those who were adolescents then remember them well, in the summer in which everyone danced "like your hands." Spike Lee uses the camera with rare mastery, and cinematographers and set designers are skilled in rendering the colors, the vibrations, and the faces of twenty years ago, besides just the clothes and cars. The film alternates the plot with the historical narration of the customs of the time. Lee succeeds brilliantly in weaving the different planes, involving the viewer in an odyssey of emotions and memories that make those two hours and twenty minutes pass as smoothly as a *cuba libre*.

The viewer doesn't know whether to shudder when the shadow of Sam wanders the dirty streets of the Bronx, or to cry listening to Thelma Houston's "Don't Leave Me This Way." One ends up doing both. In 1977 Spike Lee was a young urchin who ambled through New York with his Super 8, filming all that happened around him. New York's streets are the best film school possible. He lived in Brooklyn, where many were relieved that "Sam" was killing only whites, ideally young brunette women, who evidently were not liked by the Labrador.

And the Son of Sam? From the Sullivan Correctional Facility, near the gray capital of Albany, he is perplexed. David Berkowitz claims to no longer listen to dogs, he has converted to Catholicism, is considered a "model prisoner," and freely gives interviews to the media. He claims to pray for his victims, and also for Spike Lee and his family, who in his opinion was unwise in re-evoking those wicked actions, even though he probably has not been allowed to see the film. Berkowitz does not speak of the infamous crimes of his youth. He is always polished; photographs show him a quiet man with a serene expression. Many relatives of his victims are infuriated; they accuse Lee of profiting from their grief. They may even sue him. Certainly, a film such as this may recall that terrible pain, like Dido's invitation to Aeneas, "*Infandum, regina iubes, renovare dolorem...*" But the film captures much more: the habits, trends, and songs from the beginning of the postmodern age, perhaps, after the end of the illusions of '68. For those who were adolescents at the time, the film re-evokes the beginning of the contradiction between a world that went toward John Travolta, and another world, absorbed and slightly frightened by that just-cited Virgil.

24

Atlantic City: Gambling at a Fever Pitch

The passion for gambling is growing in America, and the industry is adjusting itself accordingly

More than twenty years have passed since the release of Louis Malle's magnificent film *Atlantic City*, which earned an Oscar nomination and international critical acclaim. These twenty years have witnessed the passing not only of Burt Lancaster, the great male protagonist of the French director's melancholy film, but also that of the other protagonist of the film, Atlantic City as it was then. Towering gray skyscrapers, adorned with bright and elaborate neon writing, indicating in lights the names of each casino and its affiliated hotel, have replaced human-scale and European-style casinos. The real and fake gangsters portrayed in Louis Malle's film would be able to resist the baroque excesses of Donald Trump (seen as the traces of a glorious yet remote past). Donald Trump has, in recent years, erected two true monuments to kitsch, so extreme as to be almost charming in their utter lack of taste: the Taj Mahal, a casino designed on models from Indian culture and architecture, and Caesar's Palace, with a façade in marble and particle board evoking the pomp and splendor of ancient Rome, something about which, as heirs to that great empire, Americans are enthusiastic. The young Sally—Susan Sarandon in Malle's film—would certainly not today leave provincial America to go to Atlantic City to be a croupier, following the dream of experiencing, even if only in its overseas replica, the glamour of Monte Carlo.

Atlantic City, as we saw it on a frigid December day, where the gray of the city was blurred with that of the sky-scraping casinos, and the red borders of a beautiful Atlantic sunset mingled with the enormous luminescent signs, is thousands of miles from Monte

Carlo. The long shoreline is dotted with seashells and gentle, frigid waves. It is a pleasant Atlantic beach, which separates (by a few dozens of yards) the huge cement casinos—decorated with Roman columns, or gigantic statues of Wile E. Coyote and the Tasmanian Devil—from the calm New Jersey waters. The streets of Atlantic City are deserted, the downtown neighborhoods are little more than shantytowns, and small, bleak houses, half-demolished, perhaps even abandoned, punctuate the spaces between one Trump triumph and another.

Inside these mega-casinos, however, swarms a whole world of curious visitors, as well as true enthusiasts. What is most striking other than the sheer size of the noisy gaming halls, as large as soccer fields, where slot machines and roulette tables alternate with a certain symmetry, is the "democratic" character of gambling in Atlantic City. The few times I have set foot in Italian casinos—where a dress code requiring a jacket is strictly enforced—they have always intimidated me, as in one particularly ridiculous experience, many years ago, in Saint-Vincent, where I went with my friend Roberto Figura, and was made to wear a jacket that wasn't mine and a tie that was, to put it mildly, eccentric. Italian casinos impose a decorous, elegant dress code, as well as, obviously, a certain atmosphere. Odd, that all this be required in order to be allowed to tempt fortune, and come out perhaps penniless, but if one has not pawned the jacket, at least properly dressed and still maintaining a *bella figura*.

In the lavish rooms of Atlantic City, any type of outfit is allowed, including a sweat suit. Champagne is not the standard (I believe there is little of it flowing, perhaps only on the upper floor suites), and neither are Cuban cigars. One relies on Coca-Cola, which, though it certainly doesn't help digest the loss of dollars, is at least inexpensive. How much time can one spend gambling at those diabolical slot machines with the amount of money that a good "Veuve" or even just a "Moët et Chandon" would cost!

Gambling fever is experiencing constant, almost exponential, growth in America. Casinos are opening all over, more and more often being granted state licenses. Las Vegas will always be the mecca, of course, even if the fact that it is now quasi-colonized by Disney makes it even more fantastically garish than Atlantic City

Atlantic City: Gambling at a Fever Pitch 141

and less "authentic." Upon hearing that, of course, one immediately wants to go there. Statistics show that soon every American will have access to a legal casino—for the many illegal ones, it's a different story—within 200 miles from home. In 1997, Americans gambled $638.6 billion in casinos, of which they lost $51 billion. Native Americans living on reservations are getting license after license to open "ethnic" casinos, and thus to reinvigorate the relatively weak economic status of some of the western states.

In 1989, according to Timothy O'Brien, an expert on the history and economics of gambling, most gambling took place in Las Vegas and Atlantic City. Now, only slightly more than half of the casinos are in those two entertaining cities. Floating casinos are the rage in the Gulf of Mexico, in Florida, and in California. They evoke the old Atlantic gaming houses of the 19th century, immortalized in many stories and by a famous episode in the adventures of Tex Willer, a popular Italian western comic book character, on the trail of Fred Brennan. What is striking is that Americans are so enthusiastic about these floating casinos that they are even building artificial basins in which to moor them. This may not be as thrilling as gambling in the middle of the Gulf of Mexico, where one runs the risk of losing everything and ending up in a desperate final swim among famished sharks, but they will no doubt supply the artificial basins with (artificial) sharks of their own, giving the desperate gambler "the thrill of the final dive."

Puritanical Americans, those who denounce the evils of gambling, can find refuge in only four states: Wyoming, Utah (that impregnable Mormon stronghold of America), Arkansas (home of Bill Clinton, who is given to other types of games), and finally Alabama. Other than that, only Alaska and Hawaii remain without casinos. In 1975 the only real casinos were in Las Vegas, while Atlantic City, though characterized by a strong secular tradition of gaming, had not yet asserted itself. Times change. The "gambling demon" triumphs. A new slot machine was invented, to be placed on an electric treadmill. Gambling has even entered the gym. There are agreements in place. One will soon be able to do exercises, lift weights, and climb those killer stair-climbers, while inserting quarters into a little machine that systematically devours them. Now you can simultaneously lose money and extra weight. This is no doubt healthier than having slot machines in McDonalds.

I know many who would be attracted to another new type of slot machine: one that would continuously play music and video footage of Elvis Presley who, apparently, is forever popular with many Americans. One might think of something similar, which would instead project videos of historical interest. But that would, no doubt, be ... a gamble.

25

A Day in the Life of Philadelphia

A city in crisis, yet full of vitality and initiative, with a charm of its own

It's difficult to be in a state of crisis—even if a subtle and long-standing crisis—when the rest of the United States seems to be enjoying a time of prosperity that has been going on for several years, and which doesn't seem about to end. Recent statistics indicate that even areas once defined as poverty-stricken and underdeveloped, such as the Appalachian mountain range, are slowly following the general trend of the country and fast disappearing as backwaters. Current research regarding the Appalachian mountains, which stretch from Connecticut to Tennessee, passing through Virginia, West Virginia, and other states, and which incidentally fostered an interesting internal subculture, and not only Dolly Parton, reveals a (statistical) reduction by half of the number of counties that in the sixties were classified as poor and underdeveloped. The Appalachians, in their timid yet seemingly unstoppable economic rebirth, pass through Pennsylvania—close, although not too close, to the proud city of Philadelphia.

For Philadelphia, abandoned in the last few decades by many of its leading industries, the year 2000 marked the bicentennial of an unhappy event, destined to change, for the worse, the future of the glorious city of William Penn and Benjamin Franklin: the country's capital was moved to Washington, D.C., seen unanimously, or nearly unanimously, by Congress as having a more strategic location, as well as one best suited to fulfill the role of "prime city" of a country which already had a clear vision of its destiny: to become the most prosperous and powerful country in the world. If Philadelphia's political prestige diminished with the decision of 1800, the year before Jefferson took office as president, the other major disgrace to befall the city (the most important and wealthiest city in America until halfway through the century) was the bankruptcy of Nicholas Biddle's Second Bank of America in 1814, due to President Andrew Jackson's attack on it. The decline of Philadelphia was sudden and steep.

While from a political point of view Washington replaced Philadelphia, its role in the country's economy was gradually eclipsed by that rising star, New York, which offered a much more convenient port from every point of view, but especially in relation to primary trade exchanges with Europe. Philadelphia was to become a city of religious tolerance *par excellence,* a garden city, as envisioned by William Penn when he founded it in 1682. It was not intended as a fortress city, as were many in those days, created especially to defend against Native American attacks. In 1844, however, Philadelphia was shaken by the famous "Native American Riots," an attack devised by Protestants (who oddly enough considered themselves native Americans, without giving much consideration to the Delaware Indians who had perhaps inhabited the region for millennia) against foreigners, especially merchants of small or middle caliber, and against Catholics, who had for some time been well established in what was supposed to be a haven of religious tolerance. In certain respects, in effect, it undoubtedly was and remained just that.

In fact, Protestants of many different denominations settled there and still have churches there. Already during the Colonial period a considerable number of Jews, a number that would become substantial in the second half of the nineteenth century, had settled in Philadelphia. The Jewish presence in the city is still apparent, attested to by its many synagogues, but also by a large museum dedicated to Jewish-American history, one of the most important in the country, and by the activities of a research center affiliated with the prestigious University of Pennsylvania. This center for Jewish Studies, directed by a renowned scholar of the Italian Jewish Renaissance, David Ruderman, every year welcomes scholars from around the globe, each of whom concentrates on a different research subject.

Philadelphia is a city that makes itself readily available to visitors; its geometrical subdivisions by streets and neighborhoods, in the shape of a sort of large lozenge, are easy to navigate. It is also a city proud of its historical monuments: the first seat of Congress and the famous Liberty Bell, which rang its fatal strokes marking the end of the War of Independence and the beginning of the great American saga. A small but interesting exhibit of documents, "Evolving Philadelphia—Transitioning for the 21st Century," at the time of my visit (April 1999), was housed in the basement of City Hall, where people file their local taxes, obtain birth, marriage and death certificates and the like; it is a modern, anonymous building right in the center of the city. There, on two walls facing each other, were documents from the Public Records Office and other documents from various other sources. The exhibition was organized by the Office of the City Representative and Director of Commerce, a government agency that serves as liaison between the local population and the city's administrative officials, with the primary duty of overseeing and making public the way in which citizens' taxes are spent. On display are documents from several interesting episodes of Philadelphia's recent past, such as the impressive "Freedom Festival" of 1981, a kind of celebration of the continued spirit of tolerance which has always characterized the city, as well as a celebration of the spirit of cultural initiative. It is no coincidence that we are talking about the city of the unique genius that was Benjamin Franklin, the spirit thanks to which, for example, a new and remarkable central theater, the Regional Performing Arts Center, was inaugurated in 1998.

The exhibition also provided interesting information about Philadelphia's economic development, which saw a resurgence in strength between the end of the 19th and the beginning of the 20th centuries, up until the Great Depression of the 30s swept away many important industries including wool and press businesses, which had flourished in the beginning of the century and had become in effect the most important of their kind in the country. The glorious National Publishing Company only recently went bankrupt, and its offices, right in the city's center, were converted into luxury apartments in 1998. Other businesses, however, have moved their headquarters to Philly, such as SmithKline, one of the largest pharmaceutical companies in America, which has its new offices in a jewel of contemporary "corporate architecture." Philadelphia also houses various art museums such as the Philadelphia Art Museum, full of splendid European masterpieces.

In April 1999, a unique exhibit opened at the Pennsylvania Academy of Arts dedicated to the artist Maxfield Parrish, an eccentric interpreter of American modernism. Throughout his long life—he was born in Philadelphia in 1870, and died in 1966 after having achieved great fame, as well as the open admiration of Andy Warhol, among others—Parrish proved to be not only a admirable example of artistic transformism, but also and especially of national popular art. His works were primarily intended to become widely distributed advertisement posters and lithographs. In the '20s and '30s he was one of the most popular artists in America and his works were celebrated, such as the Ferry's seeds advertisement depicting an angry, vaguely sensual little girl. Another celebrated ad was of a young woman leaning forward, her long black hair blowing in the wind against the background of an ominously stormy sky, a testimonial for Edison batteries. Parrish used many different techniques, but his subject were essentially few: primarily scenes of Europe, the Orient, or of tranquil New England landscapes—never, however, depicted in a realistic way, but instead transformed, rendered surreal and magnificent by the incessant and intense activity of the artist's imagination.

His art represents idylls in fairy tale landscapes and illustrations of real fairy tales with a complete domination of the expressive medium, and the (admitted) cynicism of creating art for profit and for businesses, those new and generous patrons of the arts. It is no coincidence that Parrish illustrations even accompanied boxes of candy.

Not very well known in Europe, Parrish suffered a steep decline in fame after the Second World War, perhaps because he had yielded too much to the demands of the market, and the American public was fully aware of this and did not approve. But the form of his creative process, his idyllic and fairytale worlds, never devoid of a certain subtle sensuality, his colonial gardens full of little girls and bustling and festive young women, made a comeback during the Pop Art years, as could be expected. His imaginary worlds titillated the taste of an average public, only moderately educated, who saw a realized, if not reassuring, sweetened representation of its own world in the lithographs and calendars designed by the Philadelphia artist. This master of strong, excessive, metallic, gaudy, at times almost expressionistic colors, conveyed, paradoxically, a poetic message that is truly impressionist, sentimental, and soft. Parrish was a great virtuoso with the paintbrush, who even invented a color -- a shade of blue, naturally -- which now bears his name.

He was a true American, and, in many respects, a true son of Philadelphia.

There's no doubt that the Georgian style red brick houses of Society Hill (the old "model" quarter of Philadelphia), hide within their walls many serial works by Parrish. In a certain sense, his works of art, much like the city of Philadelphia itself, embody something profoundly American, something lost in the bureaucratic chill and boring order of Washington, but lost equally in the glamour of New York City, which seems again prey to one of its periodic fevers of self-exaltation, no doubt healthy, but often not tolerable for too long. Philadelphia maintains a solid and polite discretion and uniqueness even if its crime rate is extremely high on the outskirts of the city, just over the Delaware, where the satellite town of Camden is plagued by serious socio-economic decline, and a general degeneration which is not at all visible in what was the first capital and the beacon city of the newly established United States of America. It is where remain, for many, those illusory dreams of youth, of nature and of *eros* that abound in the kind of fantastic symphony that is the art of Maxfield Parrish.

26

Vienna in New York

Stanley Kubrick and Arthur Schnitzler meet on the silver screen

The audience does not hide its embarrassment as it exits the movie theater. Outside, in the sultry air of late spring in New Jersey is the desolate spectacle of a large mall, full of cars and anonymity, of restaurants and gas pumps. Young men and women, pensive and somber, climb into large red SUVs. They remain silent while the torrid air caresses them for a few moments before returning to an artificial sense of well-being, almost immediately brought back by what resembles a liberating ritual: air conditioning. Route 14, wide and welcoming, with its four lanes and an almost continuously straight path, scatters them between New Jersey and Pennsylvania, back to the *mare magnum* of the wealthy American suburbs around Princeton, between New York and Pennsylvania. Their feeling of awkwardness is not due to the undoubted eroticism of *Eyes Wide Shut*, Stanley Kubrick's film released posthumously in 1999. These young people are used to that, and much more, simply from watching television.

The embarrassment originates instead from incomprehension. What exactly was the story about? Why was its language so strange, one which only students of German history and culture—or of psychoanalysis—could even begin to understand? How did it actually end? In short, the film introduced a series of questions that show the sense of displacement, or, to use the Freudian term, and thus to enter even further into the atmosphere of the film, the *Unheimlichkeit*, "the discomfort of being away from home." This sensation is felt when confronted with this enigmatic film, which takes its atmosphere, as well as entire lines, from a Viennese text from the 1920s called *Traumnovelle* by Arthur Schnitzler. Nothing could be further from mall-ridden and Internet-driven contemporary America. The sense of estrangement is reinforced by the casting of Nicole Kidman and her then-husband Tom Cruise, who, in the diorama of the minds of young and not-so-young Americans represent vitality and a source of life force, action and reaction, special effects and more or less healthy sensual affects. They play a couple in marital crisis, a couple embodying Viennese *Dekadenz*, following the dissolution of the Empire and all of its certainties, at a time when Vienna is no more than the political capital of a province.

It is an odd meeting, that of a director who was always very American despite his golden exile in the suburbs of London, a voluntary and not often highlighted exile, but which lasted decades, and the world of *Mitteleuropa*. That is, odd moving from a thriving and powerful empire, alone at the summit of the international power hierarchy, to a now tragically defunct empire, in its brief democratic interregnum, or thought of as such, before the *Anschluss* of 1938. This period is known as the annexation, received happily by the majority, to Hitler's Reich, another empire, but with far different and more deadly implications than the Austro-Hungarian empire under Franz-Joseph.

Adapting, or rather reversing the category coined by Edward Said, Orientalism, referring to a typically European, typically 19th-century vogue, we might speak of "Europeism" on the part of Americans (and why not of the Japanese as well?). Europeism is a mythical vision that can be, and has been, manipulated to varying degrees on an artistic, literary, ideological, and political level. The concept is Europe conceived not as what it is or what it has been in reality, but simply as it appears in the collective American imagination. This collective imagination was nourished by literature, many (although often brief) trips, and much history in the humanities departments in American universities, at least until local history, then South American, Asian, and finally African history got the upper hand. *Eyes Wide Shut* could be interpreted, reversing the literal meaning as eyes fixed on the object, and a free mental image then projected onto film, of what the eye sees in a quick blink, just before closing and re-elaborating the whole with the aid of the imagination. Could this be a general trait of American Europeism?

It is difficult to say. One needs only to stick to this particular case (of a new type, one might say, but also very old, if you think only of Henry James, although with very different outcomes). The history is, in fact, that of a twofold dream. The very blurred lines between dream and reality are traditionally present in German literature, even before the great psycho-analytic framework that runs parallel to Schnitzler, with sporadic epistolary encounters, full of reciprocal esteem and admiration (and the sense of belonging to the same vein of "research") between Schnitzler and Freud. Both were readers of each other's works yet never truly collaborators. A text that weaves wakefulness and sleep, actions carried out in consciousness and those carried out in dreams, mixed up and superimposed, is *The Prince of Homburg* by Heinrich von Kleist, a romantic poet as isolated as he was genial, who committed suicide (in a double suicide, along with his beloved) in 1811. He had been so shaken by his reading of Kant, so will we therefore never be able to know true reality, but only phenomena? The question was enough to confound the sensitive mind of a poet and revolutionary. Kant, however, does not represent the origin, but only the landing place of the thought process. The true origin is Descartes: how might one truly determine, with certitude, what one experiences in the realm of dreams and what one experiences in wakeful reality? In other words, how can one distinguish when one is awake from when one is dreaming?

Kubrick's film closely follows Schnitzler's text. Clearly, not only the screen adaptation, but also today's entertainment requirements, accentuate and carry to extremes both dialogue and situations. At times dialogue coming from the upper-bourgeois, "high" and cultured language of Schnitzler is immediately followed by the more casual language of American daily life: hurried, vulgar, without any haughtiness, what one might call "practical" language. This linguistic juxtaposition heightens the alienation of the film. Vienna is transposed to New York, in fact to an even more artificial New York, than the one Kubrick created in his London studios. The last film of a genius, then, although set in the city in which he was born (Kubrick's father was a doctor, as is the protagonist of the film and of the novella) brought no form to reconciliation between the city and the old master. New York City appears to be the cradle of every sort of perversion, precisely on the eve of a Christmas which otherwise might seem reassuring to all. The couple is fed up and is searching for an escape. It is an old and well-known story.

The woman's escapes are only dreams, figments of her imagination. She dreams of making love to many men, and with open eyes, confesses to having dreamt of being swept up in amorous ecstasy by the strong arms of a lifeguard she had met on vacation. Orgasms are described that never occurred, and yet, after the wife confesses to her husband her desire, they are visualized and concretized once again, this time in the mind of her husband, who, obsessed by never-consummated adultery, goes in search of forbidden pleasures in a moderately violent nocturnal New York. It proves to be an excursion full of surprises, all marked by a sexual relationship never actually consummated, but only, in a very Freudian manner, sublimated in its desire, so strongly as to render impossible its actual realization. So strongly or so weakly?

The situations that Bill (the film's protagonist) and Fridolin (the novella's protagonist) encounter are parallel: the temptation of a threesome at the opening party, the prostitute who discovers she is sick, the grotesque and surreal orgy, the young and perverse daughter of the costume salesman who yields to a ridiculous Japanese couple, in the best tradition, in the back-shop. The story and film travel on parallel tracks, but to where? The *pièce de resistance*, in both cases, is represented by the consummation of an orgy. In Schnitzler quite sparingly, here in baroque fashion by the followers of a sect in Venetian costumes and masks, in an improbable, spectral, neo-gothic mansion (who knows if they had already used it in some B-horror movie). The music is evocative of late medieval monastic chanting, both resounding and numbing. 18th century Venetian ornamentations, brocades, and damask fabrics, together with a priest of some pagan cult (recalling, but how much more disturbing were those! the Egyptian-style druids of Pasolini's *Salò*) make up the background of an extremely static and not particularly exciting orgy, one might say even deathly, and which concludes, in fact, not with a collective orgasm, but rather with murder. Thus, everything is a dream: life (and sex)—to agree with Calderón de la Barca—is but a dream (or a nightmare). The only thing that is real is death.

Bill/Fridolin, lured by a pianist friend, penetrates the mansion of the disciples in search of forbidden sensations, is recognized as an intruder, and would meet an unhappy end if a young priestess, statuary and courageous, does not decide to sacrifice herself for him. She sacrifices her own life in order to save that of the young, good-looking, rash, and more or less sexually excited doctor. (If he is indeed just that, for it is not clear either in the film or in the novella.) In the end, the outsider is redeemed and saved by the beautiful woman who in a way falls in love with him, and offers her life to her cult tribe. The tribe is thirsty for the blood of the invader, of the outsider who has dared to penetrate the temple of forbidden and ridiculous pleasures, assuming the garb of a disciple without truly being one. As Peter Gabriel would have sung before signing on to do soundtracks for movies about cute little pigs, "He looks like we do, he talks like we, but he's not one of us..."

The orgy ends, the morning brings revelations, and the following morning the liberating final weeping, which reunites the couple broken up by dreams that were never realized and by the misunderstanding that went along with trying to have them realized, which brings Bill/Fridolin to the confession of Albertine's "temptation," on the shores of Denmark. "Something is rotten in Denmark," we might sigh along with Shakespeare. In Denmark Albertine had suffered the wild temptation of yielding to the arms of the mysterious lifeguard, and "Denmark" is, in the novella (not in the film, which loses many of the narrative subtleties of the novel), the keyword that the friend will imprudently blurt out to Fridolin, with whom he will penetrate into the stronghold of the perverse as into a cage without an exit.

The end is an end of reconciliation, almost a Hegelian *Versohnung*, if it weren't for the foul language: there's an ironic and vital twist, utterly American, added to the finale of the film, in which the woman suggests to the man that they "do something they hadn't done in a long time," and, in response to his begging for clarification, she responds: "Fuck!" Something which, in fact, they had not done during the course of the film, as opposed to the more carnal Fridolin and Albertine, who do it from the beginning. An entirely different mitteleuropean anxiety lies in the end of the novella: The gray dawn was creeping in through the curtains when Fridolin finished [his story]. Albertina hadn't once interrupted him with a curious or impatient question. She probably felt that he could not, and would not, keep anything from her. She lay there quietly, with her arms folded under her head, and remained silent long after Fridolin had finished. He was lying by her side and finally bent over her, and looking into her immobile face with the large, bright eyes in which morning seemed to have dawned, he asked, in a voice of both doubt and hope: 'What shall we do now, Albertina?'

She smiled, and after a minute, replied: 'I think we ought to be grateful that we have come unharmed out of all our adventures, whether they were real or only a dream.'

'Are you quite sure of that?' he asked.

'Just as sure as I am that the reality of one night, let alone that of a whole lifetime, is not the whole truth.'

'And no dream,' he said with a slight sigh, 'is entirely a dream.'

She took his head and pillowed it on her breast. 'Now I suppose we are awake,' she said, '--for a long time to come.'

He was on the point of saying, 'Forever,' but before he could speak, she laid her finger on his lips and whispered, as if to herself: 'Never inquire into the future.'

So they lay silently, dozing a little, dreamlessly, close to one another--until, as on every morning at seven, there was a knock on the door; and, with the usual noises from the street, a victorious ray of light through the opening of the curtain, and the clear laughter of a child through the door, the new day began. (Translated by Otto P. Schinnerer)

All of this is more disturbing than the dismissive "Fuck!" uttered by the beautiful but cold Nicole Kidman, who, from her native Australia, captures little of Schnitzler's Austria. From the final lines one can deduce, through this all-too-reassuring dawning, that the classic little crack of the House of Usher has crept in, as per that images, not become topos, created by Edgar Allan Poe, which will (perhaps) make the entire structure, perhaps previously sturdy, collapse.

In Kubrick's finale, after real deaths and imaginary orgasms—as though the former weren't much more obscene than the latter—everything seems patched back up under the veil of an optimism that is very American and truly reassuring in the sense that it imposes, though an obscene and dismissive word, but one which in effect signifies a completely healthy activity, the end of libertine, orgiastic, mercenary, even illegal indecencies. Incidentally, these have ended up with a nice fresh corpse at the morgue, and others arriving, such as the prostitute who discovers she has AIDS or the perverse girl, daughter of the costume vender, destined for an equally unhappy fate.

Thus we witness the triumph of conjugal love after temptation, which has its basis in Saint John the Baptist in the desert, as well as Christ himself. The film emphasizes Freudian anxiety and its criticism of the institution of marriage, as if in a great American vendetta against psychoanalysts and writers seduced by Schnitzler's ideas, one can no longer take the liberty of questioning the holy, Catholic institution of marriage and precisely that which it legitimizes: screwing. Moreover, vices and perversions are projects in distant social classes and subclasses, either by excess (perverted rich swine) or by default, in the case of the underworld of prostitutes/sociology students (as can be seen by the presence of a book, *Introduction to Sociology*, lying around the squalid apartment of the prostitute who will discover that she is suffering from AIDS) or by the perverted Japanese couple who seem to have come out of a pornographic *anime* of the worst possible taste, and who, in an utterly oriental fashion, treat themselves to games meant for troubled adolescents, with a perverted Russian girl, whose social class, insomuch as it is not American, is of little interest.

All of these people, however, belong to classes and subclasses that are worlds away from the solid middle-class context of William Harford, a doctor who lives well, though not extravagantly (at least by New York standards) in Central Park West, near the Natural History Museum and the New York Historical Society. A comfortable bourgeoisie, no doubt, and much more, if we compare it, in terms of economic history, to the Viennese upper middle class of the 1920s, a period of serious crisis, not only moral, but also economic, for Austria, for the first time in centuries deprived of its empire.

Nevertheless it doesn't seem morally and intellectually permissible, when faced with a film such as this, to yield to dismissive temptation, or to join the chorus, albeit small, of fanatic enthusiasts. In reality it provoked general questioning, which is enough to place it in the small group, ever more restricted, of great works. And it is no coincidence that there are not only people involved in the film industry and in film criticism who have been talking about the film, but also intelligent historians such as Peter Gay, who has recently dedicated five large volumes to the 19th-century bourgeoisie, from Queen Victoria to Freud, and who, from his adoptive city of New York, directs the cultural programs of the New York Public Library and can deservedly comment on the last film of Stanley Kubrick. But most of all there is something about Schnitzler better known in Italy than in the United States. One can conclude that in the end it is worth rediscovering him for the pleasantness of his writing and for little else: Vienna of the early 20th century is really too distant from New York at the close of the millennium.

Schnitzler, in the words of Peter Gay, appears to be who he was in reality, and for this he could still attract attention in the United States: a real sexual addict, in continual, exhausting pursuit of female prey, with whom he had an astonishing number of relationships which he enumerated and maniacally listed by the hundred per month in his journal. He was a doctor/writer, considerably more successful as a writer than as a doctor, who certainly did not give us his best (by then he was tired, as a writer and especially as a lover) in *Traumville*, published a few years before his death in 1931. His obsession with love triangles, with marital infidelity, with erotic performances, is all in all very far from the New York of 1999, and Peter Gay's timid defense of Schnitzler's reflecting life of our times shows just how out of date he is. And here too one can find a key to understanding Kubrick's film. The testament of the undisputed master—whose life and death were coolly commented on by Spielberg without much heart at the Oscars—is a true representation, or rather meta-representation of that which is not of our time.

It is all about a game of masks, behind which true faces never appear. It is a celebration of transgression, without there ever being any real transgression. In short, it is a true intellectual game, aided by a quite haughty unreality, in the hyper-intellectual style of a writer such as Frederic Raphael, who has authored enigmatic books as well as the screenplay, somewhere between psychoanalytical and vaguely erotic, of *The Hidden I*. Kubrick left behind something of a theory. In postmodern America, every story can be adapted to film, and can represent reality, as varying as it is, and among the infinite morsels of the Big Apple of the 1990s one can no doubt find a little piece of Vienna of the 1920s. Why not? Everything is a story and, together, everything is reality. In this sense, the film is truly disorienting: it deals with sex without raising excitement, it deals with death without creating anguish, and it deals with life without offering any real slice or representation of it. It is, in short, a mystification, or rather a representation of mystification. In this respect, it has a profound effect. And, *à la* Nietszche, it is profoundly unreal. It leaves everyone lost and speechless. To seize the essence, one needs to rise to the level of Schnitzler and Kubrick. Otherwise, it is like water running on stone. And, in this America, in this desolate mall in sunny yet somber New Jersey, people wonder what exactly they have just seen, what they actually felt while seeing it.

Few, perhaps, will come to the conclusion that they found themselves confronted with a fascinating contrast between America and Europe, and between the past and the present, as only a true genius could envision. Needless to say, not without being enigmatic, as suits a genius, and for which only a genius can be forgiven.

Index of Names

Abba, 137
Abramovitz, Max, 106
Adams, Henry, 59
Adams, John Quincy, 126
Adler, Stephen, 70
Adorno, Theodor W., 51, 111
Aeneas, 138
Afghanistan, xi
Africa, xx, 28, 101, 113, 117, 120
Alabama, xii, 5, 141
Alaska, 141
Albany, 138
Alberta, 33
Alighieri, Dante, 23, 30, 116
Alpert, George, 103
Altshuler, David, 21
America, see United States of America
Americas, xv, 12, 18, 22, 29-31, 37, 64, 74-76, 91, 112
Appalachian Mountains, 143
Arkansas, 141
Arlington, 45, 46
Arnheim, Rudolf, 105
Arnold, Eberhard, 32
Asia, 113-115
Athens, xix, 19, 46, 62
Atlantic City, 122, 139-141
Atlantic Ocean, 37
Auburn, xii

Auden, W. H., 105
Auschwitz, 21, 26
Auspitz, 30
Australia, 85, 90, 119, 154
Austria, 77, 154, 155
Avinger, Joanne, 53

Bahcall, John, 70
Bailyn, Bernard, 61, 63, 65
Balkans, 127
Bamberger, Louis, 70
Baton Rouge, xv
Battery Park, 1, 21,
Baudrillard, Jean, xv
Bay Ridge, 19
Bayliss, Sarah, 46
Beall, Cecil Calvert, 46
Benzi, Rosanna, 49, 50
Bergen, Cadice, 8
Berkowitz, David, 135-138
Berlin, 25, 39, 40, 96
Berlin, Ira, 1, 3, 4
Bernini, Gian Lorenzo, 71
Bernstein, Leonard, 105
Biddle, Nicholas, 144
Bird, Kai, 131
Black Kettle, 7
Bloch, Marc, 109
Blue Ridge Mountains, 60
Boas, Franz, 3

Index of Names

Bobbio, Norberto, 96
Bolívar, Simón, 75
Bologna, 104
Bombieri, Enrico, 70
Bon Homme, 32
Boston, 38, 74, 104, 105
Bradley, Bill, 44
Brandeis, Louis Dembitz, 103, 104
Brazil, 101
Brennan, Fred, 141
Brighton Beach, 19
Brodie, Fawn M., 57
Bronx, 17, 18, 136, 138
Brooklyn, 12-14, 18-20, 136, 138
Brother, Jonathan, 46
Brown, Peter, 137
Buber, Martin, 105
Bucci, Stephanie, xiii
Buffon, Georges-Louis Leclerc, Comte de, 63
Burke, Edmund, 27, 28
Bush, George W. Jr., 44
Byron, George Gordon, 7

Caesar, see Julius Caesar, Gaius
Caffaro (Cafarus), 109
California, 41, 83-85, 104, 141
Camden (NJ), 147
Camus, Albert, 132
Canada, 31, 74, 92
Caravaggio, Michelangelo Merisi known as, 127-130
Carax, Leo, 13
Carter Brown, John, 74
Casanova, Giacomo, 38
Castiglione, Baldessar, 78
Catherine II, Empress of Russia, 74
Cavalli Sforza, Luca, 59
Cecchi, Emilio, xvii
Central Europe, 28
Central-Eastern Europe, 12, 22
Central Park, 5, 45, 47, 155

Charlottesville, 55, 60
Chic, 137
Chicago, 27, 89, 90, 128
Chin, Alan, 128
China, 28, 73, 114, 115
Chivington, 9
Chivington, John M., 7, 8
Churchill, Winston, 133
Cincinnatus, Lucius Quinctius, 43
Cipolla, Carlo Maria, 111
Clausewitz, Karl von, 61
Clinton, Bill, xi, xx, 5, 11, 57, 81, 141
Cole, John W., 93
Columbus, Chistopher, 55, 67, 75, 114
Colorado, 1, 7-9
Colorni, Eugenio, 96
Como, xii, xiii
Condorcet, Marie-Jean-Antoine-Nicolas de Caritat, Marquis de, 61
Connecticut, 29, 143
Constant, Benjamin, 64
Cooley, Robert, 57
Coolidge, Calvin John Jr., 48
Cosway, Maria, 61, 62
Coyote, Wile E., 140
Crockett, David, 46
Cruise, Tom, 150
Cuba, 23
Cuomo, Mario, 22

D'Annunzio, Gabriele, 129
Dalrymple, Louis, 47
Dante, see Alighieri, Dante
Danube (river), 13
Darling-Hammond, Linda, 79
Darnton, Robert, xvi
Davenport, Homer, 46
De André, Fabrizio, 7, 9
De Kooning, Elaine, 106

Index of Names   161

De la Barca, Calderón, 152
De La Tour, Georges, 129
De Niro, Robert, 12, 129
De Palma, Brian, 136
De Sade, Donatien-Alphonse-François, 63
DeWitt (NY), 18
Delaware, 44, 144, 147
Della Casa, Giovanni, 78
Denmark, 153
Denver, 7, 9, 77
Descartes, René, 151
Dido, 138
Di Leonardo, Micaela, 89
Dilthey, Wilhelm, 109
Donzelli, Carmine, 98
Doodle, Yankee, 46
Dutch Antilles, 75

Eastern Europe, xvii, 12
Einstein, Albert, 69, 70, 107, 132
El Dorado, 84
Elias, Norbert, 51, 92
Eliezer, Israel ben (Baal Shem Tov), 12, 13
Ellis, Joseph, 58, 59, 61, 64
Ellis Island, 21
England, xvi, 27, 43, 65, 86, 89, 96, 111, 116, 118
Europe, xv, xviii-xxi, 8, 9, 12, 13, 18, 23, 24, 28, 30, 32, 33, 42, 49, 55, 62-65, 67, 73, 74, 76, 81, 96, 97, 101, 105, 110-112, 115, 116, 119, 127, 128, 137, 144, 146, 150, 157 (*see also* Central Europe, Central-Estaern Europe, Eastern Europe, Western Europe)
Evanston (IL), 89

Ferdinand II, King of Aragon, 13
Fernández-Armesto, Felipe, 114, 116

Fichte, Johann Gottlieb, 98
Fiering, Norman, 67, 74
Figura, Roberto, 140
Fink, Carole, 109
Finkelman, Paul, 56, 57
First Lady, *see* Rodeham Clinton, Hillary
Florence, xix
Florida, 141
Fogel, Robert W., 131
Forlì, 84
Foster, Eugene A., 59
France, 19, 64, 90, 96, 116, 124
Francis, Saint, 52
Franklin, Benjamin, 143, 145
Freiberg, Jack, 11, 128
Freiburg, 67
Freud, Sigmund, 151, 156
Fukuyama, Francis, 117

Gabriel, Peter, 153
Galbraith, John Kenneth, 112
Gandhi, Mahatma, 5
Garon, Sheldon, 123
Garrett, George, 50
Garton Ash, Timothy, xvii
Gates, Bill, 110
Gay, Peter, 156
Geertz, Clifford, 70, 91, 97
Geismar, Caspar, Baron von, 64
Genoa, 109
Gentile, Giovanni, 81, 96
Gentili, Alberico, xvi
Georgetown (DC), 83
Germany, 19, 28, 67, 70, 89, 92, 96, 109, 116, 133
Gherardesca, Ugolino della, 116
Ginsberg, Allen, 47
Giustiniani, Agostino, 109
Goebbels, Joseph, 23
Goldhagen, Daniel, 25
Goldstein, Israel, 103

Index of Names

Gore, Al, 44
Gozzano, Guido, 129
Greece, 97
Greene, Nelson B., 46
Groves, Leslie, 133
Guazzo, Stefano, 78
Gulf of Mexico, 141

Habicht, Christian, 71
Haiti, 55
Hamburg, 23
Hamilton, Alexander, 43, 58
Harford, William, 155
Harrison, Wallace K., 69
Harwitt, Martin, 133
Häuser, Arnold, 105
Hawaii, 141
Hefner, Christie, 106
Hegel, Georg Wilhelm Friedrich, 22, 63, 110
Heine, Heinrich, 96
Hemmings, Eston, 59
Hemmings, Sally, 57-61
Hempstead (NY), 15
Henrietta (little girl of West Point), 4
Hertrich, William, 85
Hida, Shuntaro, 132
Hirohito, Emperor of Japan, 133
Hiroshima, 121, 131-134
Hirschman, Albert O., xvi, 68, 70, 95-101
Hirschman, Ursula, 96
Hispaniola, 55, 114
Hitler, Adolf, 26, 96, 131, 150
Hofmann, Dustin, 129
Holliwood, 106
Holmdel, 123
Hopper, Edward, 86
Hostetler, John A., 32
House Trist, Eliza, 64
Houston, Thelma, 138
Hudson River, 11

Humboldt, Alexander von, 63
Humboldt, Wilhelm von, 65
Hume, David, 61
Hungary, 28
Huntington (Henry Edward and Arabella), 83-85
Huntington, Arabella, 84, 85
Huntington, Henry Edward, 41, 84, 85
Huntington, Collis, 84
Husserl, Edmund, xix
Houston (TX), 49
Hutter, Jacob, 30, 31

Illinois, 90
India, xxi, 73, 81
Indies, 114
Indonesia, 16, 28, 98, 101
Innsbruck, 30
Iraq, xi
Isabel I, Queen of Castile, 13
Isaiah, 52, 117
Israel, 22, 106
Italy, xii, xiii, xxi, 4, 28, 52, 64, 70, 75, 77, 79, 81, 82, 93, 96, 100, 105, 107, 127, 156
Ithaca, 46
Ivory, James, 60, 61

Jackson, Andrew, 144
Jackson, Sarah, 86
James, Henry, 151
Japan, xviii, 28, 115, 116, 133
Jefferson, Thomas, xvii, 35, 42, 43, 55-65, 78, 144
Jehovah, 53
John the Baptist, Saint, 155
Johnson City (NY), 18
Johnson, Lindon, 124
Jones, Grace, 137
Jordan, Michael, 110
Julius Caesar, Gaius, 42, 109,

Kant, Immanuel, 151
Kavafis, Konstantinos, 51, 74
Kennedy, John F., xx, 5
Kennedy, Robert, 125
Keppler, Joseph Jr., 46, 47
Kertzer, David, 106
Ketner, Joseph, 105
Keynes, John Maynard, 98
Kidman, Nicole, 150, 154
King, Martin Luther, 5, 125
Kleist, Heinrich von, 151
Klimt, Gustav, 71
Knapp, Caroline, 135
Koch, Edward, 22
Kojève, Alexandre, 117
Korea, 28
Kosovo, xvii, 121, 127, 129, 130
Kracauer, Siegfried, xix
Kubrick, Stanley, xvii, 122, 149, 151, 154, 156, 157
Kushner, Tony, 27

Lady America, 47
Lady Liberty, 46
Lancaster, Burt, 139
Landes, David S., 68, 109-119
Langer, Lawrence L., 26, 27
Lankau Watts, Kelly, 124, 126
Laocoön, 53
Laos, 17
Las Vegas (NV), 140, 141
Latin America, xx, 74, 76, 98, 100, 101
Latvia, 18
Lavin, Irving, 70
Lawrence, Jacob, 106
Lee, Henry, 43
Lee, Spike, 122, 135-138
Leguizamo, John, 136
Leibniz, Gottlieb, Wilhelm, 81, 118
Lemaître, Jules, xxi
Leontief, Wassily, 36, 39, 40, 99

Levi, Primo, 26
Lévi-Strauss, Claude, 89
Lewinsky, Monica, xx, 60
Lewis, John, 4-6
Lewisohn, Ludwig, 105
Lifschultz, Lawrence, 131
Lincoln, Abraham, 47, 55-57
Lithuania, 18
Liverpool, 17, 92
Locke, John, 61
London, 150, 151
Long Island, 15
Loos, Adolf, 38
Los Angeles, 37, 83, 87
Lubin, Hannah, xiii
Luckman, Charles, 36-38, 40
Lucretius, Titus, 127
Louis XVI, King of France, 62
Lynchburg (VA), 60

Machiavelli, Niccolò, 128
Machine, 137
Madoff, Bernard, 68
Malle, Louis, 139
Malone, Dumas, 58
Mandeville, Bernard, 64
Manganelli, Giorgio, xvii
Manhattan, 12-15, 20, 21, 136
Mantegna, Andrea, 109
Manuel, Frank E., 105
Maria Teresa of Austria, 31
Maritain, Jacques, 105
Marocco, 113
Marshall, George, 97, 98
Marx, Karl, 39, 99, 111
Martha's Vineyard, xx
Mason, George, 43
Massachusetts, 45, 103
Massachusetts Bay Colony, 104
Mauss, Marcel, 89
McGillis, Kelly, 29
Mead, Margaret, 89, 105

Index of Names

Medici, Lorenzo de', xix
Meldolesi, Luca, 96, 100
Merian, Sybille, 75
Mérillion, Georges, 129
Merini, Alda, 35-36
Michigan, 90
Mickey Mouse, 47
Miller, Steve, 1, 3
Miller, Vassar, xvii, 35, 49, 50, 52, 53
Minnesota, 33
Mises, Ludwig von, xii
Mohammed, 119
Montale, Eugenio, 20, 86
Montana, 31, 33
Monte Carlo, 139, 139-140
Montesquieu, Charles Louis de Secondat baron de La Brède et de, 61, 62, 101
Montgomery Flagg, James, 46
Monticello, 60, 62-65
Moos (South Tyrol), 33
Moravia, 30, 31
Mosse, George L., 23
Mount Vernon, 41
Mozambique, 116
Münster, 30
My Lai, 8

Nagasaki, 131, 133
Naples, 77
Napoleon I, Emperor of the French, 42
Nappi, Chiara, 77-81
Nast, Thomas, 46
Nelson, Ralph, 8
Neumann, John von, 70
New Amsterdam, 21
New England, 74, 105, 146
New Jersey, 67, 69, 70, 121, 123, 125, 140, 149, 157
New World, *see* Americas

New Paltz, 19
New York, 1, 15, 17, 19, 29, 45, 46, 78, 80, 149
New York City, 11, 19, 21, 22, 23, 25, 29, 30, 37-39, 45, 55, 69, 74, 90, 104, 105, 122, 123, 135, 135, 138, 144, 147, 151, 152, 155, 156
Niebuhr, Reinhold, 132
Nietzsche, Friedrich, 39, 157
Nighthorse Campbell, Benjamin, 9
Nixon, Richard, 125
Nolte, Nick, 60
North, Douglas C., 110
North America, *see* United States of America
Novick, Peter, 26, 27

O'Brien, Timothy, 141
O'Connor, Mike, 129
O'Hara, Scarlett, 4
O'Neal, Shaquille, xix
Oceania, 116
Ohio, 42, 104
Obama, Barack, 2
Oder (river), 13
Oe, Kenzaburo, 132
Old World, 18, 29, 39, 76, 112,
Olsen, Theodore V., 8
Oppenheimer, Henry, 70
Osnabrück, 30
Ota (river), 132, 133

Pacific Ocean, 37, 114
Padova, xii, xxi
Paine, Thomas, 63
Pakistan, xxi
Paul, Saint, 32
Paqarizi, Ali, 128, 129
Paret, Peter, 61, 65, 71
Pareto, Vilfredo, 118
Paris, xix, 61, 62, 64
Parrish, Maxfield, 146, 147

Index of Names

Parton, Dolly, 143
Pasadena (CA), 83
Pasolini, Pier Paolo, 152
Pataki, George E., 22
Penn, William, 45, 143, 144
Pennsylvania, 143, 149
Pesaro, 84
Peter the Great, Emperor of Russia, 73
Peters, Victor, 32
Petrusewicz, Marta, 98
Peynet, Charles, 60
Philadelphia, 69, 104, 122, 143-147
Pizzorno, Alessandro, 99
Plato, 136
Plutarch, 36
Pocahontas, 41
Poe, Edgar Allan, 27, 154
Poland, 12, 13
Pony, Ashley, xiii
Poplar Forest, 60, 63
Portugal, 76
Poseidonia, 74
Praz, Mario, xvii
Presley, Elvis, 137, 142
Princeton, xi, xvi, 67, 97
Providence (RI), xv, 5, 67, 68, 74

Queens, 136

Radin, Paul, 3
Raphael, Frederic, 156
Rawls, John, 132
Rhode Island, 5, 74
Rhodehamel, Peter, 42
Riedemann, John, 31
Rimbaud, Arthur, 13
Robinson, Yvonne, xiii
Rockwell, Lew Jr., xii
Rodeham Clinton, Hilary, 44
Romano, Sergio, xiii
Rome, 19, 46, 109, 139

Ronan, Richard, 50
Roosevelt, Eleanor, 105, 106
Rosenthal, Mel, 15-20
Roosevelt, Franklin Delano, 47
Rotblat, Joseph, 132
Rothbard, Murray, xii
Rousseau, Jean-Jacques, 61, 62
Ruderman, David, 144
Rusconi, Claudia, 98
Russell, Bertrand, 132
Russia, 18, 31, 73

Said, Edward, 150
Saigon, 125
Saint Petersburg, 36, 39
Saint-Vincent (Aosta, Italy), 140
Sainte Marie, Buffy, 8, 9
Salter, Mary Jo, 61
Sampson, David A., 50
San Andreas Fault, 84
San Felice (Val di Non, Italy), 93
San Francisco, 125
San Marino (CA), 41, 68, 83, 84
Sand Creek, xvi, 1, 7-9,
Sandy Creek (river), 7
Sarandon, Susan, 139
Sarna, Johnatan, 104
Schaefer, Peter, 25, 28
Schinnerer, Otto P., 154
Schneck, Bill, 46
Schnitzler, Arthur, 149-152, 154-157
Schorsch, Ismar, 11
Schumann, Robert, 53
Seattle, xix
Selma (AL), 5
Sen, Amartya, 97, 99
Shakespeare, William, 86, 153
Shapiro, Louis, 105
Simmel, Georg, xix, 98
Singleton Copley, John, 86
Sisyphus, 101
Skrabala, Lauren, xiii

Index of Names

Slovakia, 31
Smith, Adam, 99, 110, 113, 118
Smith, John, 41
Sobibor, 27
Sombart, Werner, 98
Son of Sam, *see* Berkowitz, David
Sorvino, Mira, 136
South Africa, 113
South America, 21, 73, 74, 96, 119
South Dakota, 31-33
South Tyrol, 33
Soviet Union, xviii, 18, 77, 113, 133
Spain, 13, 76, 97
Sparta, 62
Spielberg, Steven, 27, 156
Spinelli, Altiero, 96
Sraffa, Piero, 98
St. Louis, 26
Staden, Heinrich von, 71
Steele Scott, Virginia, 86
Stella, Frank, 106
Strauss, Peter, 8
Streep, Meryl, 24
Sudetes, 28, 90
Suharto, Haji Mohammad, 16
Swan, Claudia, 1, 128
Swan, Jon, 1, 29, 32, 33
Switzerland, 116
Sydney, 25
Syracuse (Italy), 19
Syracuse (NY), 19

Taiwan, 115
Tasmania, 119
Tasmanian Devil, 140
Tennessee, 143
Texas, 4, 49
Theresienstadt, 23
Thomas, Dylan, 105
Thompson, Therry, 125
Tillich, Paul, 105
Tönnies, Ferdinand, 31

Tracy, Destutt de, 62
Travolta, John, 136-138
Treblinka, 27
Tret (Val di Non, Italy), 93
Trieste, 96
Troy (NY), 5, 45, 46
Truman, Henry, 126, 133
Trump, Donald, 139, 140
Tunisia, 113
Tyrol, 30, 92 (*see also* South Tyrol)

Ugolino, see Gherardesca, Ugolino della
Uncle Tom, 4, 57
Uncle Sam, xvii, 35, 45-48
United States of America, xi-xiii, xv, xvi, xviii-xxi, 1-4, 6, 8, 9, 13, 15-20, 22, 23, 28-33, 35, 38-47, 49, 55, 56, 62, 64, 67, 68, 73, 74, 76, 77, 80-82, 84-86, 89, 92, 93, 96, 97, 99, 101, 104, 105, 107, 110, 111, 115-119, 121, 122, 124-127, 133, 137, 139-141, 143-147, 150, 156, 157
U.S., *see* United States of America
USA, *see* United States of America
USSR, *see* Soviet Union
Utah, 141

Val di Non, 90, 93
Ventura, Lino, 136
Venturi, Franco, 97
Victoria, Queen of the United Kingdom, 156
Vienna, 149-151, 156, 157
Vietnam, 8, 9, 17, 47, 121, 123-125, 137
Virgil (Vergilius Maro, Publius), 138
Virginia, 4, 41, 42, 75, 90, 143
Voltaire, François-Marie Arouet known as, xix, 62

Vouet, Simon, 128

Waldner, Johannes, 33
Wallace, George, 5
Walpole, Horace, 64, 119
Waltham, 103, 106
Waltner, Emil J., 33
Walzer, Michael, 70
Warhol, Andy, 47, 146
Washington (DC) xix, 4, 7, 23, 33, 35, 55, 83, 124, 144, 133, 143, 147
Washington, George, 35, 41-44, 55, 69, 78
Weber, Max, 98, 111, 118
Weir, Peter, 29, 30
West Point, 4
West Virginia, 143
Western Europe, 127
Weyden, Roger van der, 128
White, Morton, 71
Who, 137

Wiesel, Elie, 21
Wilde, Oscar, xiii
Willer, Tex, 141
Williams, Roger, 104
Wilson, Samuel, *see* Uncle Sam
Wiesenthal, Simon, 26
Wolf, Eric R., 68, 89-93, 117
Wood, Gordon S., 42-44, 61
Woodstock, 125
Wyoming, 141

Xerxes I of Persia, 119

Yamahata, Yosuke, 132
Yorktown (VA), 43
Young, James E., 25
Yugoslavia, 121

Zerubavel, Eviatar, 111
Zevi, Sabbatai, 12

www.ingramcontent.com/pod-product-compliance
Lightning Source LLC
Chambersburg PA
CBHW031313150426
43191CB00005B/217